UNSTOPPABLE

UNSTOPPABLE

7 SIMPLE STEPS
TO GET UNSTUCK,
MAKE THE BIG CHANGE,
AND UNLOCK YOUR POTENTIAL

MICHELLE BONAHOOM

UNSTOPPABLE: 7 SIMPLE STEPS TO GET UNSTUCK, MAKE THE BIG CHANGE, AND UNLOCK YOUR POTENTIAL

Copyright © 2019 Michelle Bonahoom

ISBN: 978-1708714246 (print)

Also available in Kindle format on Amazon.com

Cover design by Yvonne Parks at pearcreative.ca
Typesetting by Katherine Lloyd at theDESKonline.com

Printed in the United States of America

20 21 22 23 24 6 5 2 3 2

Contents

Chapter I

WHY UNSTOPPABLE?

What would happen if you made one big change in your life? I have spent my career asking that question of leaders as I help them navigate critical transitions in their lives. I have been a business owner for almost twenty-five years. For thirteen of those years, I worked in and with over one hundred companies and their leaders as they fought for survival, struggled with the challenges of growth, bought and/or sold, and transitioned to the next generation of leadership.

During this time, I have come to realize that high performance and growth don't happen without embracing conflict and intentionally seeking big changes. I've also learned that conflict and big change can feel overwhelming and complicated, leading most people to avoid them, question what they should be doing, or—even worse—stay stuck where they are. But the reality is that growth won't happen without change, and it takes dying to old ways of doing things for new ways to take root. This can be distressing when there is no roadmap to follow along the way.

My goal is to give you the tools you need to become unstoppable. What this means in your life is that you gain the ability to successfully walk through the changes and transitions that come as you journey from where you are to where you want to be.

More than that, these tools will help you identify where you want to be with enough clarity that you will be able to start mapping the steps to get there, and that you will feel compelled to keep moving in that direction until you achieve your goals. You will become resilient, able to withstand the inevitable unpredictable things that come up along the way. You will become unstoppable, able to make targeted choices that launch a series of events leading to your goal, like a chain of dominos expertly set up.

Setting up dominos can be tedious, but what you accomplish by simply tipping over that first domino can be incredible. In one of my workshops, I give attendees one normal-sized domino. Then, at some point, I have a volunteer come to the front, where I have set up a series of dominos. Each domino is larger than the one before it, and the final domino is one hundred pounds. When you compare the normal-sized domino to the last one, it seems impossible that one small domino could ever topple the largest one, yet because of the domino effect, it can and does.

Each domino's fall contains enough energy to move something larger than itself, which means each one falling can topple something greater. This is the same power our choices have. The potential energy of one choice can quickly lead to impact greater than we originally thought possible.

This is how change works. One intentional act leads to big change in our own lives, which then affects the world around us. A transformation of our choices leads to personal transformation, then our individual transformation leads to group transformation—whether that group is work, family, or friends—and that group's transformation leads to community transformation. This is the power of choice.

Through the years, I have looked for ways of making this process simpler and more impactful. I have been a change agent of sorts my entire life. When things began to feel complacent or uninteresting,

I would seek the next mountain to climb. I have lived life accepting the fact that growth doesn't happen without intentionality and embracing the conflict that comes with change. During those seasons of change, I have recognized principles and patterns that cause people to embrace the conflict associated with change, intentionally seek new ways, and successfully navigate the journey.

My Unstoppable Story

In January 2017, I began to write in my journal about the anticipation of breakthrough that was coming that year. I wrote about the necessary endings that would come and the new season that was ahead. I started to position my life for big change with an excitement that I had never had before.

Can you relate to this? Have you ever felt something was the New Year's resolution that you were *finally* going to achieve, the turnaround that was now within reach? Have you ever had the anticipation of a new life, despite where you currently were? This was me!

I spent that year declaring a new day was coming, planning what the end result would look like, and starting to walk out what I thought was my future reality. During the year I posted and blogged about courage, shifting seasons, letting go of the past, active peace, rising up, and laughing at the storms.

Then, in August 2017, I felt a prompting that it was time to write the book—this book! I wrote in my journal, "Don't write the big book yet, things are still unfolding for you. Write often and pointed. Write with building blocks. Speak! Identity is key. Build foundational resources." After years of preparation, reflection, and application of the principles and tools, I thought I was ready to sit down and knock it out. It was *finally* time to share these universal and timeless principles with the world, and I could hardly stand it. Little did I know that I was about to embark on the greatest journey of change in my life (to date).

The week of September 24, 2017, started out like most. It was filled with anticipation for the change that was coming. I had written in my journal that this was a week of major breakthrough. I couldn't wait to see what change was coming! I was scheduled solid with work, leaving little margin for meaningful relationships or health. I was certainly not practicing what I preach as a coach who believes in whole-life health. I was overcommitted at work and in ministry, was trying to manage the busy lives of four active preteens/teenagers, and hadn't been taking care of myself.

My husband and I were passing each other without connection as we ran four different directions at any given time. I was three hundred and fifteen pounds, dealing with multiple diagnoses (high blood pressure, diabetes, high cholesterol, sleep apnea, hormonal imbalance, endometriosis, and allergies) and was on seven medications. Needless to say, I would come home and go right to bed.

On Thursday, September 28, I taught at a women's ministry school I was helping to lead. My topic was on being a lifelong learner. I spoke about overcoming limiting beliefs, knowing who we are, setting our lives on a solid foundation, and then declaring the truth until we believe it. I equipped the women with several of the transformational tools that I would be writing about over the next several months.

I came home late—tired, hungry, and conflicted—and wondered if what I had taught was *really* true because someone had challenged it that night. I had even stopped at Taco Bell to get lots of cheap food to console me. I walked into the bedroom and turned on the lights, which woke my husband, Rob, and caused him to go to the basement to sleep. Angry that he didn't even say hello, I proceeded to drown my fears and insecurities in tacos. I tossed and turned all night, questioning the truths I had declared, feeling guilty, and wondering if true transformation was really possible.

On Friday, I was exhausted, as I got up at the crack of dawn to push through another day. I had finally made it to Friday and was looking forward to coming home, vegging in front of the television, and eating my worries away. Rob was feeling the pressure of our lives too, so we were looking forward to spending time over the weekend "getting our life in order." The last words I said upon leaving my final meeting that day were, "I am so glad it is Friday! I am *so* exhausted. At least it can't get any worse than this. Something needs to change."

I pulled in my driveway and took one last call before the weekend started. Something felt off, but as I looked around everything seemed to be in order. Kids were playing in the yard, Rob's car was in the garage, and everything seemed normal. Little did I know, in a few short minutes, my world would drastically change.

As I got out of my car, my eleven-year old daughter frantically ran out of the house, saying, "Come quick! Something's wrong with Dad!" Somehow I knew this night was about to get much worse.

I walked in the door and immediately saw that our lives had shifted forever. Rob had unexpectedly and peacefully passed away from what we would later learn was undiagnosed heart disease. In an instant, I found myself not just facing all the problems that had kept me up and exhausted me the night before, but now also grieving the loss of my husband—widowed, unsure of where we were financially, and needing to care for and support four grieving kids, all while managing two businesses that weren't stable enough for me to back off temporarily. Having spent the last thirteen years walking beside business owners and leaders as they navigated critical transitions, I knew that over 50 percent of all transitions happen because of unexpected events like this, yet I still was not prepared for what was ahead of me.

This was a huge wake-up call. Without warning, I was confronting the perfect storm where every area of my life was facing critical change. So I turned to what I knew. I pulled out my journal and compiled a list of every promise, encouraging word, dream, and insight that I had written down over the past ten years (that was how long I had been keeping a journal). I put those words in one place and started to look for themes. Then I pulled out the transformation model tools and resources I had been using to walk clients, friends, and family through transition over the last thirteen years. My only way out would be to practice what I preached.

Fast forward about twenty-four months and I am sitting here excited to tell you about the significant breakthrough I have had since that life-changing day. *Every* area of life has been transformed, despite it being the most challenging season of my life.

For example, the week before Rob passed, I had written in my journal, "You are ready. The trial will prove your faith. It is time to fly." I had dreams that I was driving through a storm, but that my dad was in the driver's seat and showed no fear. I also dreamed that people were coming around me to support me and I realized I needed to learn how to accept that support. My faith has always been a big part of my life; however, it wasn't until I was faced with so many uncertainties that I needed to grab on to the certainty of my faith.

I realize faith may play a different role in your life, but when you are faced with uncertainty, having an anchor to keep you grounded in the middle of the storm is critical. My trials over the past twenty-four months have proven my faith, and being able to look back on over twenty-eight pages of promises, dreams, and encouraging words have been the anchor as I have navigated the storm.

At the time of this writing, I have lost over one hundred pounds. I have gone from a size 24W to a size 14. I still have about fifty pounds to go to get to my goal weight, but I no longer focus on the scale. Rather, I concentrate on living a balanced and fit lifestyle of healthy eating, exercise, mental strength, and overall wellness. As a result, I have completely reversed my diabetes, normalized my blood pressure and cholesterol, and reduced my triglycerides from 276 to 78. I am off all my medications and have more energy than I had in my twenties. The best part is that I am able to do normal things that many people take for granted, like ride a roller coaster with my son or fit in an airplane seat without having to ask for a seatbelt extender. And—for you ladies—I am finally able to shop in cute boutiques and wear skirts and tall boots for the first time in years!

So many other areas of my life have also transformed. My relationships are entirely different. My relationship with my kids is the best it has ever been, and they are also now role models in their own groups. And others who have watched me walk through this process have been inspired to start their own journey.

I have seen a complete transformation professionally as well, with a new ability to assess my strengths and weaknesses and develop teams to allow me to take necessary rest. My mindset about finances has changed, growing in how I think about investment and generosity. And of course, everything related to my personal development couldn't be more different; I'm actually developing *myself*.

How did I do it? I turned to the same transformation model, tools, and resources I had been teaching business owners and leaders for years. The week after Rob passed, I pulled out my templates and started mapping out how I was going to make it through the biggest change of my life. I started with the most critical area—my health—and then worked in layers through the other areas over the course of twenty-four months. In the images below, you can see a sample of one of the plans I put together for focusing on my health.

VisionOne Transformation Model

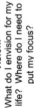

Mission:
What is my purpose? Why is this important?

My mission is to walk beside the transformation of **individuals, organizations, and communities** through **identifying the gold and leveraging the full potential** of people, so they are able to leave a **lasting legacy.**

This is important, because when people are living their best, they are able to bring out the gold in others. My role in this will lead to big impact and making a difference in the world.

Change Desired:
What change do I need to make? Why is this important?

To lose 150 pounds and be a healthy role model for my kids.

- Lose weight
- Go off medications
- Reverse diagnoses
- Be a healthy role model for my kids and others
- My health is a huge wake up call!

Vision:
What do I envision for my life? Where do I need to put my focus?

My Vision for 2019 is to demonstrate, **unstoppable faith and courage** in all areas of my life. (See vision board)

- **Health:** fit and healthy; lose 150 pounds
- **Family & Relationships:** Foundation; relationship with kids; revival
- **Spiritual:** Grow in gifts; Faith before fears
- **Personal Dev:** Confidence, playfulness & rest
- **Financial:** Overcome limiting beliefs
- **Professional:** 80% of time creative & strategic visionary; release Unstoppable

Desired Outcomes:

What are the desired outcomes of this change?

- Lose 150 pounds
- Reverse diabetes, high blood pressure, sleep apnea, fatigue, and all other diagnoses
- Be a healthy role model for my kids and others
- Be healthier than in my 20s
- Where skirts and tall boots
- Fit in a roller coaster

Values:
What value filters need to guide my life?

- **Faith:** in unseen, risk, hope, not my own strengths, declaration of past testimonies
- **Authenticity:** vulnerable, practice what I preach, proactively tell stories, embrace failure
- **Wonder:** open, "what if?", childlike, address limiting beliefs, foster wonder in others
- **Advocacy:** bring out gold, ceiling/floor, identity, champion, overcoming, advocate
- **Impact:** Chinese bamboo, don't settle, new measures, impact beyond you, solutions two generations out!

Guardrails:
What MUST happen or CANNOT happen as I walk out this change?

- It needs to be sustainable and fit into my life
- It can't require lots of time and prep.
- It needs to involve REAL FOOD.
- I can't be based on lack.

VisionOne
HIGH PERFORMANCE GROUP

VisionOne Transformation Model

Purpose:
Why do I need to change?

☐ Be available for my calling
☐ Be there for my kids
☐ Overcome the one area of my life that has kept me stuck

Principles:
What mindsets need to change?

☐ My weight is hereditary
☐ It took me 20 years to put it on...
☐ I can't take this on during this season!
☐ I am alone

Practices:
How do I change?

☐ Prayer, gratitude, and declarations
☐ Diet, supplements, and detoxing
☐ Exercise
☐ Emotional healing

Proficiencies:
What *skills* need to be *mastered* to maximize the change?

☐ Diet - fasting, cellular healing lifestyle, and supplements
☐ Exercise - "Joyful Movement"
☐ Mindfulness – "follow the bread crumbs"
☐ Delegation!

Platform:
What *support, resources* and *accountability* will ensure sustainability?

☐ Transformation Team: Wellness Coach, Personal Trainer, Chiropractor, Doctor, Therapist, Massage Therapist, Coach (business and life), and Prayer Team
☐ Friends, Family and Team
☐ Meal and exercise plans; Green Chef
☐ Lifestyle vs. Diet

Performance:
How will *I know* I have met my goal?

☐ 90 day challenges
☐ Biometrics and blood testing
☐ Weight and clothing
☐ How do I feel?
☐ Feedback from others

VisionOne
HIGH PERFORMANCE GROUP

9

An Unstoppable Guided Journey

Walking through my own journey of practicing what I preach is what became the platform for *Unstoppable* and the beginning of this book. I had been teaching this for years, but it wasn't until it was tested in my own life that I was able to see its simple, universal, and timeless transformational power to make big change seem simple. As a result of my own journey, I have organized this book as a guided journey for you to take as you navigate your own change(s) in life.

Let's face it, change is hard. But not changing is harder, and the steps to change can be simple. If you engage with this guided journey, it will help you:

- Stop chasing symptoms and solve the right problem
- Go after your change for the right reasons
- Reverse limiting mindsets that are preventing change
- Establish habits that will lead to desired results
- Surround yourself with the right support systems, tools, and resources that will help sustain your change
- Set relevant measures and learn to celebrate the little wins instead of getting discouraged when change gets frustrating

This first chapter's intention is to tell you my story of navigating critical change in all areas of my life. I have come to realize that our stories have transformative power. The breakthrough I have experienced is available to you just by reading about it. You get to start at the place just beyond where I left off, so take my testimonies and claim them for your own life. We are different people. Your circumstances and desired outcomes may be similar to or very different from mine, but my breakthrough can be a starting place that drives momentum for yours.

Then, having read about the potential of these tools, chapters two through eight will guide you on the journey of how to implement these tools in your own life. Each chapter will cover one of the seven P's of transformation:

- **Purpose**—Clearly defining your change, desired outcomes, guardrails, and true purpose for the change
- **Passion**—Having a strong foundation in place (mission, values, and vision)
- **Principles**—Identifying the mindsets, blind spots, limiting beliefs, and strongholds that need to change in order to unlock, realize, and sustain your change
- **Practices**—Defining what you need to do differently in order to build new habits for change
- **Proficiencies**—Maximizing your change by building the knowledge, competencies, and skills necessary to master your desired outcomes
- **Platform**—Building the culture, support structures, tools, and resources necessary to help you successfully carry out and sustain your desired change
- **Performance**—Celebrating wins, measuring results, and adapting to new levels of success along the way

Each chapter is broken down into four sections: *context, assess, align,* and *apply.* The context portion will help you understand why that transformation principle is important, provide research to substantiate the importance of the principle, and include an example from my own journey to serve as a platform for you to launch from.

The assess section will be a place for you to reflect on where you are at with each step. By understanding where we are at, we can go where we need to go. In this section, be sure to focus on the attitude and emotions that rise up inside you. These are like a warning light on your dashboard. They will help point to the root fears that may be causing you to avoid change, the areas that are keeping you stuck, and the places you should be aware of as you engage in that area of change.

The align section will outline three to five keys that will help you be more successful with your change. It will also be backed up with stories from my life and the lives of clients, family, and friends who have experienced transformative change in their personal life or in business as a result of this transformation model.

Finally, the apply section will be an opportunity for you to put your change to action. Part of this model includes the "show, do, teach" method, which is one of the most powerful ways to strengthen and retain the transformation you want. It will also enable you to see the benefit of this process in the lives of others. There will be a variety of other practical and powerful actions you can choose from as well.

While this same model can be (and has been) used to transform families, businesses, and communities, transformative change can't happen until you start within yourself. The greatest leaders know they cannot sustainably change their families, teams, businesses, or communities until they have first changed themselves. However, as you walk through your own change, my hope is that you are inspired to use these principles, tools, and resources to change the world around you.

Getting the Most Out of Unstoppable

All this may seem intimidating at first, but the good news is that we are wired for success![1] Plus, the more you focus on the right

---

1 Dr. Caroline Leaf, *Think, Learn, Succeed: Understanding and Using Your Mind to Thrive at School, the Workplace, and Life* (Grand Rapids, MI: Baker Books, 2018), 81.

mental activities, the more your brain and body will respond in positive ways. Below are several keys for successful, sustainable change:

- **Unique Identity**—This is intended to be a guided journey for anyone who wants to make meaningful and sustainable change. We are all wired differently, so different questions will resonate with different types of people. Answer the questions that speak to you and let go of the ones that don't. Pay attention to which types of questions you avoid, as these could be pointing to some areas of fear or limiting beliefs.

- **Layers of Process**—Go through this process in layers. There is a lot of information in this book, and it may take a while to draw out all the information that you need to take each step of the transformation process. That's okay. Taking time to work through this content in layers will be far more affective over time than rushing through the content as quickly as you can, thinking that because you read it, then you have done it.

- **Meditation and Reflection**—Making time for contemplative thought is surprisingly one of the most powerful things we can do.[2,3] All it takes is about seven minutes per day to begin rewiring your brain for change. One of the greatest benefits is reduction of stress.

- **Practicing Gratefulness**—Gratitude has incredible power as a catalyst for change. Similar to how, after you buy a car, you start to see many other cars the same color as yours, gratitude trains your brain to notice

---

2   Ibid., 48.
3   Ibid., 48.

the good things happening around you that otherwise might go unseen. This then brings mental-health benefits, resilience, and a general feeling that life is worth living.[4]

- **Journaling and Declaring**—Writing things down brings a different level of commitment and changes your brain. What you write moves from being a concept to being a belief, and from being a mindset to being a habit. It becomes a memory stone that you can draw from when times get tough (as I did with my ten years of journals), and declaring aloud what you want to think about or how you want your life to be has a similar effect.[5]

Your Unstoppable Story

To put it plainly, this book is not intended to be read once and put on a shelf. I encourage you to use it as a guide as you walk through critical changes in your life both now and in the future. Change is not an event but rather a journey; therefore, read through the book in layers. Come back to each chapter over and over. Download the templates, tools, and resources to navigate one or multiple changes. Reflect on the questions that resonate in the moment, come back to others later, and shelve the ones that don't seem to fit. For me, the principles, methods, and tools have become a regular part of my everyday decision-making process. Some of the tools I use regularly, while others have become

---

4   Ibid., 85.
5   Dr. Caroline Leaf, *Switch On Your Brain: The Key to Peak Happiness, Thinking, and Health* (Grand Rapids, MI: Baker Books, 2013), 73.

so ingrained in my way of thinking that I no longer need the template or tool to guide me.

Finally, have fun with the journey. Laughter will actually help you in the process of transformation, so whenever you can find something to laugh at along the way, indulge yourself![6]

If this process is stressful at any point or you feel stuck, then walk away from it and come back later. Remember, change requires conflict. Some conflict is necessary and healthy, while some is not. Pay attention to where you are getting stuck and give yourself permission to take breaks along the way, but never stop moving forward!

Looking back, it comforts me to see that I have been prepared for this journey for years. I can see that, despite my breakthrough coming in a different package than I would have ever imagined, it was in fact a breakthrough. My wake-up call has become a gift as I have walked through critical transformation in my own life and have walked beside others in their own journeys.

I feel that, in some way, this is my second chance. My hope is that as I live the rest of my days, I would purpose to be worthy of the second chance I have been given. My wish is that as you read each chapter, you are inspired to take steps toward a big (or little) change in your own life. I hope that it provides you the framework, tools, and resources to guide your journey despite the fears and pressures that you may be facing. I have faith that the stories of transformation you read along the way will be seeds that inspire you, light a fire within you, and activate similar transformation in your own life.

Finally, I hope to hear about the transformation that is happening in your families, work, schools, and communities as a

---

6   Dr. Caroline Leaf, *The Gift in You: Discovering New Life through Gifts Hidden in Your Mind* (Nashville, TN: Thomas Nelson, 2009), 216.

result of the transformation inside you. It just takes one reason, one mindset change, one intentional step, one new skill, one advocate or support structure, or one new way of measuring success to be the tipping point for change in your life.

There's really no excuse not to change, so let's get started.

Chapter 2

PURPOSE

What Is the Change
and Why Is It Important?

Every January I go through the journal I have kept for the past ten years and reflect on all the change that has happened. I dream about the future, set new goals for my year, and come out re-energized and ready to run.

I am not alone in this desire to reset, re-engage, and grow. If you were to step into any gym during this time of year, you will likely see an increase in membership and energy. For most, the renewed energy lasts for a few weeks and then returns to the old normal. This has been the case for me in multiple seasons of my life. Many of my good intentions don't seem to last. As I look around me, I notice the same—the gym is quieter, my clients go back into their old ruts, and the excitement about change dies down. Can you relate?

Why is it that despite the momentum of change, it falls off so quickly? The answer is, change is hard. Old behaviors and patterns form emotional, psychological, and neurological resistors to change that make it difficult to push through when "life" happens.

In his book *Change or Die,* author Alan Deutschman reports that 90 percent of the time when doctors say a person needs to "change or die," the necessary change doesn't happen.[1] Even when their life depends on it, only 10 percent sustainably change.

For the last three years, I have been committed to raising that statistic. Even though I've taught change for over sixteen years, it wasn't until I faced my own health crisis while also walking out the most painful season of my life that I realized how helpful this model can be to help me change so I wouldn't die prematurely. If we can't manage change when our life depends on it, how will we ever manage change in the less-critical seasons of our lives? Why do we need to wait until we get to that place where we need to change or die?

Key questions you need to ask to help with this are: What is the specific change I am trying to make? What is the problem I am trying to solve? What are the desired outcomes of my change? What do I need more of or less of? What are guardrails? What must happen and what cannot happen? Why is this change important? What is the cost of not changing?

Why Change? Why This Change?

Without change people start to die. Science shows that our brains continue to form new neural pathways and patterns throughout our lives. However, if we stop changing—forming new ways of thinking, engaging new ways of doing things, learning new skills, etc.—we start to deteriorate. Fifty percent of people who live to

---

1   Alan Deutschman, *Change or Die: The Three Keys to Change at Work and in Life* (New York: HarperCollins, 2009).

be eighty-five years old develop dementia, but those who keep changing improve their chances of staying healthy by 50 percent.[2]

Just because people don't change doesn't mean they can't change. We already saw that fear of death is not a strong motivator for change, but tying that change to something meaningful today is. It is okay if that does not make sense, because as it turns out, change is not a rational process.

Gallup studies show that 70 percent of all change initiatives fail because they lack one of the following ingredients:[3]

- **Purpose and Passion**—Clear vision of the change itself and what we want to come from it, understanding of how the change will impact us or our organization, and alignment with our underlying needs and purpose.
- **Principles**—Buy-in to commit to the process or the right mindset needed for the change to happen and be sustainable. Belief systems need to change for facts to be relevant. Until our beliefs change, we internally question the source of the fact. So, if we are told that we need to change or we will die, we will not believe it until our underlying beliefs change.
- **Practices**—The right activities and positive reinforcement of the habits that are necessary to drive the outcomes needed. Radical change is typically easier for most people than small or gradual change because it leads to faster and more-noticeable results.
- **Proficiencies**—The right skills necessary for change. Too often people focus too much energy on changing

---

2   Ibid.
3   David Leonard and Claude Coltea, "Most Change Initiatives Fail—But They Don't Have To," *Business Journal*, May 24, 2013, https://news.gallup. com/businessjournal/162707/change-initiatives-fail-don.aspx

their weaknesses, instead of building on the few critical strengths that will drive the change they desire. This leads to fatigue and mediocre results that stifle the momentum of change.

- **Platform**—Support systems, tools and resources, and communication with key people. Change is not a rational process. Behavioral and attitude changes, creating new habits, and building new skills require a lot of emotional support.

- **Performance**—The ability to measure, align to, and realize the results necessary to drive the desired change. What gets measured gets done, which means the wrong metrics get us off track from our change; prevent us from celebrating progress along the way; and cause us to get stuck, quit prematurely, or not know when to pivot.

The reality is, of course, most of us don't actually want to die, but we get so overwhelmed with the emotions, fears, and pain associated with the change process that the benefit of the change does not seem worth it in the moment. When we align our change to something that is meaningful today, however, change becomes simple.

This is why we tend to see big change happen in times of crisis. Think about the events of 9/11. This crisis pulled an entire nation together to make big change. Our international strategies and relationships changed overnight, but changes happened immediately in every community throughout the country, large and small. In an instant, everyone dropped the labels that had divided them and united under the label of being proud Americans. Problems were solved. Relationships were healed. Life itself was given more meaning. This shows us that meaningful change happens when it is tied to something that is tangible today.

Fear of Change

Fear of change prevents most people from even getting started. The opposite of fear is love and acceptance, which means that most fear is the result of a lack of feeling loved and accepted (by ourselves or by others). Some fears are common enough to be worth covering here.

The first fear is feeling powerless where we succumb to a victim mindset. While there are some situations where we truly become victim to a circumstance, we still at a minimum have a choice to control our emotions and responses to those circumstances. We may not like the outcomes or the circumstances surrounding someone else's choice or the consequences of a particular situation, but we always have a choice in how to respond. And that is the point, so we know we always retain the power to change.

Martin Seligman, the founder of positive psychology, found that those who were not stuck had different ways of viewing the world and themselves. Instead of falling into learned helplessness, where someone subscribes to a life of misery and hopelessness because they believe there is nothing they can do about their circumstances, these people focused on what was working and what they could do. They believed that when someone retains control of themselves and their circumstances, positive results were possible, regardless of circumstance or environment.[4]

The full truth is, in fact, that our brains create our realities. It is not what happens to us in life that determines how we feel or respond; it is how our brain perceives that reality. Brain science

---

4   Henry Cloud, *Necessary Endings: The Employees, Businesses, and Relationships That All of Us Have to Give Up in Order to Move Forward* (New York: HarperCollins, 2011), 55.

has proven that our perception of our circumstances and environment controls our body, which changes how we react. Therefore, when we take control of our lives and intentionally avoid a victim mindset, our biology changes, impacting our mental and physical health.[5]

What environment, circumstances, or mindsets are preventing you from changing? How do your circumstances and environment cause you to feel like a victim, feel hopeless, or feel powerless? You can learn to recognize these feelings by listening for the places where you say, "I can't..." "I shouldn't..." "If only..." or "But..." If those powerless words come up, try reversing them with, "What if I can..." "I will..." or "How could I approach this situation differently?"

Another common fear that arises, when attempting a change, is the fear of failure or success. This is called the "failure to launch" syndrome. Our fears of failure and success keep us stuck in patterns that need to come to an end in order to get to a new normal.[6] This typically is driven by either a need to get it right or a fear of vulnerability.

While attempting to prove that vulnerability was weak, researcher Dr. Brené Brown discovered that vulnerability was actually the doorway to creativity, innovation, and wholehearted living.[7] Both creativity and innovation, by default, mean breaking from the pack to do something that's never been done before. That will always involve risk, and the core of that risk is vulnerability: Will my creation be rejected? Will the market receive my innovation? Every creation or innovation involves essentially standing before a crowd to be judged.

5   Leaf, *Switch On Your Brain*, 20.
6   Cloud, *Necessary Endings*, 11.
7   TED, "The Power of Vulnerability | Brené Brown," *YouTube*, January 3, 2011, https://www.youtube.com/watch?v=iCvmsMzlF7o.

Wholehearted living is the same. Disappointment causes many people to wall off their heart to defend against pain, but every part of our heart that we wall off against pain also becomes walled off from every positive emotion we long for and need. We cannot have sustainable change without vulnerability.

Finally, another common fear is the failure of letting go of the past. In order to change, we need to end something that isn't working and choose something else that is better. This can show up by either staying in a circumstance for too long, being defensive about old ways and habits, or changing too slowly. Typically, we do not let go of the past because our mind has developed the hardwiring that causes us to behave automatically, which creates a stuck reality where it becomes normal to be stuck and live with the situation, rather than intentionally saying goodbye to the past and hello to a new reality.[8] For this reason, we need to be intentional about letting go of the circumstances and mindsets that cause us to be stuck, and consciously and intentionally purpose to create a new normal in our lives.

I have helped companies accelerate their growth and turn around their performance for over sixteen years. In the past I recommended the "boil the frog" method of change. This method presupposes that if you put a frog in water and gradually turn up the heat, it will eventually cook without feeling the heat. Essentially, this method prevents you from facing and letting go of what needs to change in order to jump into something new.

I quickly learned that this method of change was never as effective, because people would stay stuck in old ways for too long, limiting the energy, momentum, and victory of diving headfirst into change. We tend to fear radical change because we feel it. However, radical change is easier than small or gradual

---

8   Cloud, *Necessary Endings*, 54.

change. This has been proven again and again during times of crisis when people are motivated to rally, come together, attempt big change, and celebrate tangible short-term wins that sustain the energy for big change over time.

Change Drives Conflict—Both Healthy and Unhealthy

If letting go of the past and moving into the future prevents death and is the primary catalyst for growth, then why do most of us tend to avoid it like the plague? Because most of us are averse to change. Statistically, 67 percent of the population is wired with a behavioral style that seeks safety and security.[9]

If a person views conflict as unsafe, they will naturally try to avoid it at all costs. However, effective change does not happen without conflict—without something dying or breaking down to build something new. Unfortunately, most people view conflict through the lens of fighting, winning and losing, a prolonged struggle, and incompatibility. However, conflict can also refer to a race or struggle through leading, guiding, directing, and enduring.

Healthy conflict is normal. The poet Hillaire Bellaire has written, "All men have an instinct for conflict: at least all healthy men." Why is it important to embrace the positive aspects of conflict? Because focusing on the negative aspects can be devastating! Eighty-five percent of U.S. employees report experiencing unhealthy conflict and spend 2.8 hours per week dealing with it. Thirty-one percent of managers think they handle conflict effectively, yet 78 percent of employees disagree.

At the same time, 75 percent of employees report positive outcomes from healthy conflict that would have not been

---

9 Target Training International, www.targettraininginternational.com.

realized without the conflict. In fact, 95 percent of those who have received training on conflict say that it is the biggest driver of success. However, most employees will not receive training on conflict. According to the U.S. Centers for Disease Control, now more than ever, job stress poses a threat to the health of workers and, in turn, the health of organizations, costing employers over $300 billion per year. Clearly, it is critical that people learn how to embrace healthy conflict and mitigate unhealthy conflict.[10]

The primary goal is to increase understanding with self and others, find common ground through setting clear expectations, find the best overall result for all, and intentionally seek to resolve unnecessary unhealthy conflict through addressing, reversing, and holding it accountable for change. Healthy conflict focuses on valuing individuality and authenticity, creating a safe place, getting to the root of a challenge or problem, building relational capital, having freedom from control and punishment, strengthening others, loving, and taking risk. It fosters awareness of root issues, eliminates problems from festering, highlights what is important, requires creativity, challenges assumptions, leads to better solutions, builds confidence, and develops leadership maturity.

A practical example of fostering healthy conflict is regularly asking, "What's working, what's not, and what needs to change?" This posture opens us up to continuously looking for new ways of doing things, eliminating the defensive response that can come with failure or what is not working, and seeking new possibilities.

By contrast, unhealthy conflict is abnormal. It focuses on expecting sameness, lack of transparency, lack of harmony,

---

10 Statistics from American Psychological Association; Center for Disease Control; Northwestern Mutual Life; 2008 Global Capital Report; 2008 Global Capital Report; Harvard Law School report on managing conflict.

keeping issues at the surface, damaged relationships, control and punishment, sabotage, hating, and avoiding risk. The primary causes of unhealthy conflict are extreme work demands, misaligned behaviors and rewards, overcontrol, ineffective management, unsupportive work environments, and lack of job security and trust. This unhealthy conflict leads to fear, defensiveness, guardedness, and avoidance of change.

You can spot unhealthy conflict in yourself and others when you see fear, mistrust, staying stuck, and control. For example, giving constructive feedback through a heart of helping someone to bring out the good within them and get to a better place would be an example of healthy conflict. In contrast, giving constructive feedback to support your own agenda, steer, or put someone down (intentionally or unintentionally) would drive unhealthy conflict. Healthy conflict always results in growth, while unhealthy conflict does not lead anywhere good.

There are three primary types of conflict that will emerge as you engage change: conflict within yourself, conflict with others, and conflict with your task/role/organization. We often think the conflict is with somebody else, when in reality the conflict is within ourselves or the role we are playing. However, we are wired for the dynamic tension of conflict, which means that inner tension in ourselves, with others, and with our tasks/roles/organizations that we often misunderstand as unhealthy conflict, is really the healthy tension that is necessary to keep us moving forward, changing, and growing.

What are some of the conflicts that rise up as you think about your change? What are the roots of those conflicts? Within yourself? With others? With your role/organization? Pay attention to these conflicts as you navigate through the rest of the chapters, and focus on turning them into healthy conflict that leads to sustainable growth and lasting change.

Stages of Change

It is important to proactively embrace healthy conflict and mitigate unhealthy conflict in our lives. However, what is healthy conflict at one stage of our individual or organizational development may drive unhealthy conflict in another. For example, as a toddler it is healthy conflict to fall while trying to walk. If we were to never let a toddler fall, they wouldn't learn the necessary skills to be able to walk on their own. It would also create belief systems and fears that would prevent other stages of development that are necessary in the future. However, if a teen were still falling while trying to walk, this would be unhealthy conflict because walking needs to have already been established by that point.

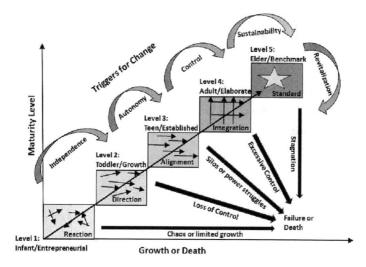

This model shows the various stages of development, whether it is individual (infant, toddler, adolescent, adult, and elder), leadership (infant leader, toddler leader, adolescent leader, adult leader, or elder leader), or organizational (entrepreneurial, growth-oriented, established, elaborate, or benchmark)

development. Regardless of the type of development, individuals, leaders, and organizations go through these five lifecycle stages throughout their lives. Each of these stages have necessary healthy conflict that needs to happen and unnecessary unhealthy conflict that needs to be eliminated in order to get to the next stage and prevent stagnation, failure, or, in some cases, death.

Infant

The infant stage is where there are many possibilities, ambitious plans, and lots of activity and hard work. There tends to be very little consistency and ability to do things on their own. Infants in this stage need to be carried. You wouldn't tell an infant to cross the street. This would be unhealthy conflict that would lead to disaster. Rather, you would carry them across. If you are in the infant stage of your change, be sure to find someone who can help "carry" you through this stage of your journey. Who are the leaders in your life who can show you how to accomplish what you want? What are the best practices that you can start to learn and follow?

When I started writing this book, I was an infant. I had never done anything like this. I tried to do it on my own but found I was getting stuck and not getting off go, so I hired a writing coach to help me through the process. He gave me a framework, provided best practices, and, most importantly, encouraged me whenever I got stuck or discouraged. Essentially, he was carrying me across the street.

I didn't have to know what I was doing. I just had to show up for the calls. Also, my discouragement was healthy conflict in this stage, because it got me to uncover and get rid of many of the limiting beliefs that would have prevented me from being able to even write and publish this book. Had I not leveraged this healthy conflict in this stage, it would have become very unhealthy conflict as I progressed.

Toddler

The toddler stage is where you start to have awareness of your potential. You believe you can do no wrong and won't fail. Everything becomes an opportunity, and you start to grow and develop. However, because everything is a possibility to a toddler, they tend to get distracted easily and don't always have the skills necessary to make the best decisions. The healthy conflict that rises up in this stage could look like a lack of focus, taking on too much (big dreams), or having unclear expectations. This is healthy in this stage, because it keeps you dreaming, trying new things, and moving forward without proven results. By contrast, unhealthy conflict at this stage would be no controls or boundaries, trying to take on too much, or overfocusing on dreams without a plan.

As a toddler, you don't want to try to cross the street on your own. Rather, you would want to grab the hand of someone older and wiser to lead you across, someone who can give you autonomy to try new things but enough boundaries to keep you safe. This can look like mentors, coaches, or others who have gone before you to make the change you are desiring. It can also look like proven systems, processes, or programs that help guide you through your change.

For example, when I set out to lose one hundred and fifty pounds, I had some experience with losing weight in the past. However, I had never lost one hundred and fifty pounds, so I found groups of people who had lost more than one hundred pounds and checked in with them regularly. I was able to add value to them and vice versa through my journey.

Adolescent

The adolescent stage is where changes start to feel out of control because so much is happening. Growth is happening, you may have multiple focuses, and you are starting to see the results of your change. This reactivity and lack of focus was healthy in the younger stages, but it becomes unhealthy in this stage because it causes confusion, overwhelm, and lack of alignment. In this stage, you need to focus and be selective about what to change. If you don't, unhealthy conflicts of priorities (internal and external) will rise up and you will start to feel out of control and unbalanced. Unlike the toddler who needed to have their hand held while crossing the street, an adolescent needs to have some freedom and autonomy to continue growing, while at the same time being restrained by a somewhat-loose rope.

I remember getting to a place in my weight-loss journey where I was simply overwhelmed. I had to build a habit of tracking what I was eating and drinking, how much I was exercising, how I was handling my emotional health, and more. I was working more and feeling inundated by it all. The focuses and tracking became overwhelming.

I realized I had moved to the adolescent stage of my journey, because what was once healthy conflict was now feeling overwhelming. So I simply focused on exercise. This is because the rest had become habit and I only needed to control what was still out of control. I had matured in my ability to eat and drink well and control my emotions, but I still needed someone to walk with me through my exercise routine.

Adult

The adult stage brings renewed clarity of vision and balance between priorities. You start to sustain without lots of focus on specific changes. New opportunities and changes rise up as stabilization of old ones happens. You form lasting habits that sustain your change. During this stage, it is healthy conflict to recognize and reinforce right and wrong behaviors, to fear letting go of control, and to lack motivation or engagement in your change. These all keep you focused on continued growth and prevent stagnation. In contrast, it is unhealthy in this stage to try to grow too fast, not stop and celebrate your progress, or not allow yourself to stabilize. All of these will lead to an inability to integrate or balance your change with the rest of your life, causing a loss of momentum and energy for continued change.

You can recognize yourself in this stage when your change has become a regular part of life. For me, it was when I hit my one-hundred-pound weight loss. I had many of the habits necessary to keep the weight coming off gradually over time. However, as I started to put more focus on other areas of life, I stopped celebrating my progress and started to feel fine with one hundred pounds despite the goal of one hundred and fifty. This was a sign that I was starting to go backward in my goal and that it was time to move into the elder stage of my journey.

Elder

The elder stage is where you achieve sustainability. There is strength in your new habits without having to focus so much on them. Your actions are guided by vision, meaning, and clear purpose. You have the right mindset around your change, are regularly setting stretch goals, have clear priorities, and are regularly putting the necessary support systems in place. You know when your change is working and when it isn't, and you have clear evidence of sustainable growth.

Best of all, your change is inspiring others to change. You have truly become a role model for people to follow in the area of your change. However, the elder stage doesn't last forever. Unless you continue to find a way to become an "infant" in a new area of your change, you will start to revert or die. This is the prime place to be. This is not a destination, but a point where you recognize that you need to find something else to change.

Whereas stabilization in the adult phase was normal conflict, it would be unhealthy conflict in this stage. In my weight-loss journey, I had become a role model for many who were trying to lose weight and get healthy. However, I started to revert to old ways because I had been too comfortable and was starting to settle. Therefore, in order to continue my journey toward health, I am now going back to some of the basics that got me to where I am today. I am tracking my nutritional intake again. I am journaling more. And I am getting involved in communities who have lost over one hundred pounds. In order to remain an elder, we need to revisit being an infant to revitalize and reenergize ourselves for the next level of change.

ASSESS: Where Are You At?

Think about the change you want to make.

- Why do you want to change?
- What fears rise up as you think about your change? Fear of being powerless or hopeless? Fear of success or failure? Fear of having to let go of something?
- What unhealthy conflict might prevent you from making this change? What healthy conflict could you embrace to help you change?
- How ready are you for the change? What stage of maturity are you at with your change?
- What emotions rise up as you think about this change?

ALIGN: Keys for Success

Now that you have the foundation for starting to navigate change, you can start by defining the change you want to make. People often try to change without taking the time to define the change they are making. Worse yet, they don't clearly define the desired outcomes of their change or the guardrails to work within, or count the cost of not changing. This leaves them going down a path without a GPS and leads to unnecessary wrong turns, frustration, and failure.

Desired Change

Start by defining the change you want to make or the problem you are trying to solve. It is important to clearly define your change so you are focused on solving the right problem, identifying the right scope, and getting to the root that is preventing you from changing.

For example, before Rob died, I was overfocused on growing my business. As a result, when the kids needed something, they would go to him. This wake-up call helped me realize the importance of building stronger relationships with my kids and helped me define my desired change as growing my relationships with my kids individually and collectively.

It wasn't until I quantified the importance of that desired change that I could fully step into defining the right change. As humans, we are wired to continually seek increased goodness and value.[11] Therefore, once you have defined the change you desire, think about how achieving that goal will drive more value in your life or organization, or the lives around you. For me, the desire to improve relationships with my kids was rooted in the

---

11 Robert Hartman, www.hartmaninstitute.org.

value of relationship. My mission to bring out the gold in others needed to start with my family. If I wasn't adding enough value to my relationships with my kids, I wasn't living my mission of bringing out the gold in them.

Once you understand the value you are truly trying to drive with your desired change, you need to get to the root of what is preventing that value from being realized. In my case, the root was that I wasn't adding enough value to my kids' lives, which manifested through the symptoms of them going only to Rob for help and my lack of relationship with them. Too often, we focus on solving the symptom and don't really get to the root of what is driving that symptom.

Once I dug into the root of what was causing our relationships to be less than desired, I was able to focus on the most important change that would achieve the results I wanted. Because of this, it is crucial to focus your change on the thing that will drive the greatest amount of value. Often we get caught up in "scope creep," where we either make the scope of our change too narrow or too broad. Making the scope too narrow prevents us from really getting to the root of our problem, while making the scope too broad causes us to miss out on the important elements of the problem, get too distracted, or end up stuck or overwhelmed, leading to failure or quitting. When you try to do too many things, you have too many brain pathways fighting each other and it overwhelms the whole system.

We are wired for winning. If you can manage one brain pathway fighting, the others will flow in that direction.[12] One way to identify the root is to look back on your life (or the life of another) and see where you had the same, or similar, result that you are seeking with your current change. For me, I was able to

---

12 Dr. Caroline Leaf, www.drleaf.com.

look back to when I did have great relationships with my kids. In every case, the root of that great relationship was connection. Therefore, I was able to focus my relationship goal on building more meaningful connections with my kids.

Desired Outcomes

Once you have defined your desired change and identified the root that was preventing it from happening, you need to make that change specific enough to sustain and focus you during the storms of life that will rise up through your change. Science has proven that setting a goal alone does not automatically improve performance, because the behavior that brought success had likely been inadequately reinforced. However, when the goal is understood and addressed properly, performance results can be increased by as much as 58 percent.[13]

This process starts by visualizing the change you want to see. For smaller changes, simply start by asking yourself, "What do I want more of?" or "What do I want less of?" Be sure to focus on the critical few things that will get you to your goal, so you don't become overwhelmed. For bigger changes, I encourage you to go through the process of creating a vision board—a visual collage of pictures and words that represent your desired outcomes. (You will go through a process to define your vision in the next chapter, but this is a good preliminary step.)

Often, we get stuck because we are trying to get things perfect throughout the various stages of change. Just like pruning a tree helps the tree accelerate growth and produce fruit, we need to prune our options throughout the process. The best way to do

---

13 Aubrey C. Daniels and James E. Daniels, *Performance Management: Changing Behavior That Drives Organizational Effectiveness* (Performance Management Publications, 2004), 241.

this is to go with what you know and shoot for 80 percent instead of perfection. So just take a stab at the first three to five desired outcomes that come up. Typically, those are the ones that really matter at the end of the day.

For me, as I imagined what improved relationships with my kids looked like, I saw us intentionally connecting, dreaming together, and laughing and having fun, and them coming to me in the good times and bad. I saw them wanting to bring their friends home to hang out. And I saw us impacting and ministering to others, both intentionally and through our normal actions. I realized that in order to achieve this vision, we needed to have more connection (intentional time), more dreaming, more laughing, and more fun. I needed to have less judgment (which meant not caring about the house being a mess for a season), less need for control (yes, even in a season where my life felt out of control), and less focus on work (despite the fact that my business needed more of my time, or so I thought).

Once you have a clear vision for how your change will look once it's accomplished, the next step is to clearly define the change you desire to make through setting SMART goals. (We will discuss SMART goals in greater detail in the next chapter.) A SMART goal simply defines your desired change based on a specific action, with measurable and attainable outcomes, that is relevant to the goal and your mission, vision, and values, with a defined and reasonable timeline. By setting SMART goals, you can set realistic expectations for your desired change.

Therefore, rather than setting a broad goal of "improving relationship with my kids," I set a SMART goal: In 2018 (*timely*), the kids and I will increase connection (*specific*) by spending more time together, laughing and dreaming together, and having more fun (*measurable, attainable, and relevant*). By setting this

SMART goal, it took the constant pressure of having to loosely grow in relationship and focused it on intentionally spending time together, laughing and dreaming, and having fun. A big, nebulous goal suddenly became simple and defined.

Finally, once you have this SMART goal defined, you will make sure it is aligned to the mission, values, and vision we will work through in the next chapter. If any part of the goal contradicts any of those, you will need to relook at your goals.

Guardrails

Once you have defined your desired change and identified your desired outcomes, it is important to set clear guardrails. Guardrails provide boundaries to work within. They answer the questions, "What must happen?" and "What can't happen?" and become a set of decision-making filters that help you know what to say yes or no to.

When I walk leaders through change, this is often an area that most struggle with. People avoid making a plan for change and setting boundaries because they don't like to be confined. After all, we are wired for freedom, growth, and possibility! However, we can't actually operate in freedom unless we have boundaries, because they filter out the static that can come with change. We live in a world where the options, opportunities, and possibilities are increasing every day, and too many options can be overwhelming.

Remember what I said about the power of pruning? There are many good options, but there are very few great ones. By limiting some of our options, we can increase our ability to harness our need for freedom, growth, and possibility. It is important to focus on the critical few (three to five) boundaries that are true non-negotiables.

I like to use the analogy of rubber, plastic, and glass balls. Rubber balls are the ones that if you drop them, they will bounce back. They aren't critical. Plastic balls, on the other hand, won't bounce back. In fact, they will roll away and get stuck under the couch, taking time and energy to retrieve them. However, glass balls are critical. If you drop them, they will break. So what are the glass balls you need to protect as you change? What are the plastic balls you need to pay attention to so they don't get lost? And what are the rubber balls you can let go of?

For me in building relationships with my kids, my glass balls were about connection time. I had to make sure we had intentional time that didn't involve me telling them what to do. I could no longer overfocus on work, so I set a guardrail that I would not work more than forty hours per week. My plastic balls were the balance between individual time with the kids and collective time. In the past, Rob and I were able to give the kids a lot more individual attention. With it just being me, I needed to find ways to bring the kids together while still giving them their time. We did that by incorporating individual time when we got together as a family. Each person had a time to have the floor. My rubber balls were the house and all the details of life that were coming at us. I needed to look away when I came home and the house was a mess or a chore was missed (I am still learning how to turn my head to this one!).

As you move through your change, you will need to test the guardrails along the way. Change is an emotional process, so things will rise up as you walk through the process. Watch for these areas of emotion to show up. Pay attention to what your glass, plastic, and rubber balls are throughout the journey. As well, different levels of maturity require a different level of guardrails. If you are new to something, you might need tighter guardrails than when you are more mature, so be willing to adapt your guardrails as you go.

Purpose for the Change

Like defining a vision for your change, it is also important to define the purpose (mission) for your change. This purpose becomes the anchor that keeps you grounded when the storms of life come up during your change—and they will come up! The purpose for your change considers why the change is really important and counts the cost of not changing.

Knowing why your change is important will drive the internal motivation that you need to get unstuck, and to make and sustain your change over time. It will also drive out the external shoulda-coulda-wouldas in life that prevent you from making meaningful change. You will end up being driven by purpose instead of emotion.

The most practical way to get to your core purpose for the change is to ask yourself the Five Whys, which I explain more in the next chapter. Start by asking yourself why the desired change is important, then take the answer and ask why that is important. Repeat approximately five times (you may need more or fewer). Often when a person finally articulates that core purpose, he or she is suddenly and unexpectedly moved emotionally. Another way to know you have gotten to your core purpose for change is when your answer lines up with your life mission.

I am reminded of a time when I was guiding a group of leaders through the process of transitioning from being supervisors to becoming owners. The group was working on defining their professional development plans. One man was having a hard time with the exercise because he started out with very surface answers. His answers kept taking him to a deeper place than a supervisor of a manufacturing company was used to going (darn that soft stuff!). After a few rounds of *whys*, he choked up when he realized that his purpose for change was rooted in being a role model for his kids. For someone who originally had a belief system that he needed to separate work from home, this was a life-changing discovery that ended up switching the direction of his development plan and transforming him as a person.

Too often, people try to keep change at a surface level or don't place value on bringing their whole self into the process. However, our subconscious can't separate circumstances. Therefore, who you are at home needs to be the same as who you are at work. Why is this important? Because if you don't allow your true, authentic self to come into this process, you won't ever make meaningful and lasting change. By getting to the root of your *why*, you can start on a solid foundation that will help you sustain your change through the challenges you will face along the journey.

The same was true in my own crisis. I had tried to lose weight for over twenty years to no avail. I had even said that it would likely take something big to get me to wake up (words I wish I would have never said). Little did I know that it would take me losing my husband, hitting rock bottom with my health, spreading my relationships way too thin, living in fear over money, and being completely overwhelmed for me to get to that place.

What was the catalyst for me? Aligning my purpose for change to something meaningful and right in front of me.

APPLY: Key Questions & Activation

Define the Change

- What problem are you trying to solve, or what change are you attempting to make?
- How have you tried to solve it in the past? What worked? What didn't work?
- What specific goal you are trying to accomplish?

Desired Outcomes

- What are three to five key desired outcomes of your change? Can you visualize them? Are they SMART (Specific, Measurable, Attainable, Relevant, and Timely)?
- How do these desired outcomes leverage your core values? Lead you toward your vision and mission?

Guardrails

- To make your desired change, what must happen to keep you on track, and what cannot happen that will derail you? (What glass balls do you need to make sure don't drop? What plastic balls do you need to make sure you don't lose sight of? What rubber balls do you need to consider letting go of?)
- How will you communicate your guardrails to others so you can have the support you need?
- How will you measure your guardrails so you know they are effective in keeping you on track?
- Test your guardrails. Are they really the critical few guardrails? As you test them, do any new guardrails emerge?

Purpose for the Change

- Why is the change needed? What value will making this change add to your life?
- What is the cost of not changing?
- What are one to three key takeaways from this chapter that you need to share with somebody else? Teach at least one other person about these takeaways.

Go to www.wearetheunstoppable.com to find simple and practical tools that can help you make and sustain your change.

- Download worksheets that will help you clearly define your desired change, identify your most critical desired outcomes, set clear guardrails, and align to a meaningful purpose for change.
- Register for online courses on healthy conflict, setting SMART goals, and driving change.

Chapter 3

PASSION

What Is My Foundation for Change?

There is an old parable that contrasts a wise man who built his house on a rock with a foolish man who built his house on the sand. The truth of this parable is still valid today: we can build any structure we want, but without a foundation it will fall when tested by a storm.

Before you attempt to make any change, it is important to have a strong foundation in place so that when hard times come, you have an anchor to keep you in place. This foundation is also necessary when you face a myriad of opportunities, options, and decisions—especially in a world of too many options—so you can stay true to who you are.

A building's foundation is usually made of steel and concrete, but the foundation for our lives is made of a clearly defined mission, vision, and values. Taking the time to define these will help us understand our purpose, place guiding boundaries to keep us moving in the right direction, and articulate targets that will enable us to both make and measure progress.

I'll tell you up-front that this chapter will require heavier lifting than any of the others in this book, but please take the time to complete it. The other chapters will help you build an amazing house, but that house will stand strong only if you have established the right foundation.

In his paper *A Theory of Human Motivation*, psychologist Abraham Maslow proposed that healthy human beings have a certain number of needs, and that these needs are arranged in a hierarchy, with some needs (such as physiological and safety needs) being more primitive or basic than others (such as social and ego needs). He suggests that the highest two needs of humanity are self-actualization (becoming the best version of ourselves) and transcendence (coming along side of others to do the same). Without achieving these higher needs, life lacks fulfillment and meaning. It is true that we could use the other chapters to improve our life in many ways, but the only way to meet these higher needs is by taking the time to define our purpose, place guiding boundaries on our decisions, and articulate targets to keep us moving forward.

Finally, a quick point of clarification. Some people interchange the terms *mission* and *vision*. I use Jim Collins's definition of mission being purpose (the *why*) and vision being what is focused on (the *what*).[1] However, it doesn't matter what definitions you use. What matters is that you have a *why*, a *what*, and a set of decision filters (your values).

Mission

The key questions your mission should answer are: What is the purpose for the change? Why is it important? The Japanese have

---

1 Jim Collins, www.jimcollins.com.

a concept called *Ikagai*, which roughly means "a reason for being."[2] As you can see in the picture, the image overlaps what you love, what the world needs, what you're good at, and what you're paid for. This concept helps us clearly see the components that make up our mission. Simply put:

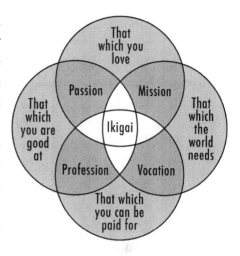

Your mission = what you love + what the world needs

Personal mission statements are an important component of business and personal development. They force us to think deeply about our life, clarify its purpose, and identify what is truly important to us. Personal mission statements also force us to clarify and express, as briefly as possible, our deepest values and aspirations. They imprint our values and purposes in our mind so they become a part of us.

Integration of your personal mission statement into your daily planning is a great way to keep your vision constantly in front of you. As well, by having a clear mission, you will not get off track from your purpose when life's circumstances change. Your mission should be timeless and not dependent on circumstance.

For example, my mission is to transform individuals, organizations, and communities by bringing out the gold in and leveraging the full potential of people so they are able to leave a lasting legacy. This statement gives me energy. It excites me. I can recall it when I am tired and it helps pull me out of bed and launch me into my day. Your mission should be able to do that for you as well.

---

2 en.wikipedia.org/wiki/Ikigai.

One of the best tools to begin defining your mission is called the Five Whys. Start with a question. I started with, "What gets me up in the morning?" Answer the question, then ask yourself, "Why?" until you feel you have found what really drives you. It usually takes about five whys to reach that point. This is how that looked when I did it.

Question: What gets me up in the morning? Answer: Leading big impact.

Why does leading big impact get me up in the morning? Because it shows me that I am making a difference in the world.

Why is it important for me to make a difference in the world? Because I want my life to have meaning.

Why is it important for my life to have meaning? Because I am inspired by digging out the gold in others and being a role model for my kids and others.

Why is it important for me to be a role model for my kids and others? Because I know my legacy will continue beyond me.

Why is it important for my legacy to continue beyond me? Because that tells me my life had meaning.

You can see that twice I came back to wanting to know my life has meaning. Yes, I was able to dig a little further to help articulate what it means to me that my life has meaning, which was good and helpful. This clearly is the root for me. Any statement about my purpose has to help define how I will feel fulfilled in knowing my life has meaning.

Then I simply took bits and pieces of my answers from Five Whys and put them together to form my mission statement. I want to lead big impact, so I say my mission is to transform individuals, organizations, and communities. I'm inspired by digging out the gold in others, so I added that to my statement as well. That is how simple it can be to articulate a powerful and meaningful personal mission statement.

Now, once you have your personal mission statement written down, test it against circumstances. I asked myself, "Are there any circumstances in life that would prevent me from living toward this mission?" No, I can always be bringing out the gold in myself and others, modeling, and providing structures that make it easy to realize full potential and legacy.

ASSESS: Where Are You At?

Now it is your turn. Think about the change you want to make. Pay attention to the emotions that rise up, as you are reflecting. Like a dashboard on a car, these emotions can be great clues to what is important, what is challenging you, and any areas that might need further reflection.
Ask yourself:

- What gets me up in the morning?
- What am I most energized about?
- What am I passionate about?
- What tells me that I am fulfilled at the end of the day?
- What is my reason for living?

Don't rush yourself while answering these questions. It is completely okay to pause here, grab a journal or your computer, and give yourself time to get clarity about these important questions. Believe me, I have walked people through this process for nearly two decades. Take the time to get this process started in the right direction.

ALIGN: Keys for Success

Answering the above questions will begin to give you the raw material you need for your personal mission statement. Before you start crafting your statement, however, double check your answers against the following statements. This will help ensure your mission statement will accomplish its purpose.

- Your mission statement should describe what it is like for you to feel fulfilled. It should spark passion and give you energy.
- Your mission statement should be a combination of what you love and what the world needs.
- Your mission statement should be timeless and circumstance-less. Test it against circumstances. If your circumstances radically changed, would you still have your mission?
- Your mission statement is internal (intrinsic), not external (extrinsic). Use the "choke-up" test (in other words, when you explain it to others, does it get you choked up?) to determine if you have gotten to the root of your mission.

This is one of my favorite exercises to take leaders through, because it is such a powerful experience to realize your personal mission! Often, leaders will start out by trying to make their mission statement fit their work conditions. However, they inevitably bump up against the fact that we can't subconsciously separate our personal selves from our roles in life (work, home, ministry, etc.).

I remember taking a new supervisor through this exercise recently. He was in one of our programs that was guiding him through learning how to become a business owner. His grid for leadership had been telling others what to do and coming behind to pick up the pieces because nobody could do it quite like him. As he started down the path of defining his mission statement, he was expecting phrases like *work hard, be responsible,* and *efficiency.*

However, he was surprised because as he worked through the Five Whys, he kept coming back to being a role model for his family. Initially, he struggled with that. How did being a role model for his family equate to being a great supervisor or business owner? However, for him it made all the difference in the world! From that moment on, everything shifted for him. He was more intentional as a leader, and the mundane of his daily work life suddenly had more meaning. He had identified his core purpose!

APPLY: Key Questions and Activation

This is the step where you will craft your personal mission statement. Use the following questions, but remember, you can skip questions that are not helpful to you. Don't feel pressure to answer every one. Instead, use the ones that spark your imagination and creativity, and the ones you feel pulling words that define your purpose from inside you.

- What gives me energy that gives meaning to my life?
- On my best day, what happened?
- What do I love that I feel called to share with others?
- If there were no obstacles (money, health, etc.), where would I spend my time and energy?
- What talents do I have that the world needs?
- What am I living for, or what do I want to be remembered for?

Use the Five Whys to get to the heart of your mission. Too often, we keep it at a surface level. Circle the key words that stick out through the Five Whys. These will be clues as you write your mission statement.

Now, take your answers and all the insights you have gained up to this point and use this template to write your mission statement:

My life purpose/mission is to: _____
_____ (what you will do)
by _____ (how you will do it), so that
_____ (the legacy you will leave).

Test your mission statement by telling a few other people. If you cannot remember it, then it is either too complicated or it does not truly resonate with you. Keep it simple and relevant. Those who know you well should confirm that your mission statement fits you, but in general, don't worry about what the world thinks. Your mission is meant to inspire *you*, as it is *your* reason for living! We all have different reasons for living.

Core Values

The key question for your core values is: What are the three to five core values that will guide all your decisions?

Core values are the fundamental beliefs of a person or organization. These guiding principles dictate behavior and can help people understand the difference between right and wrong. Core values also help individuals or companies determine, by creating an unwavering guide, if they are on the right path and fulfilling their goals. Like your mission, your core values need to be timeless and not dependent on circumstance. When applied to all your decisions in life, they become a litmus test for being able to say yes or no, which keeps you on solid ground and moving in the right direction. When articulating your core values, keep in mind:

- Values are the primary filters in life that help guide your decisions and actions.
- Values are the guiding forces that tell you and others what you stand for.

- Values are different from good attributes.

Core values are so important for effective and sustainable change because all conflict, whether internal or external, is a result of conflicting values and the perceptions of those values. People make thousands of conscious and subconscious decisions every day. Those decisions are solely based on what is viewed as being more valuable or not. Therefore, by having a clear set of core values to filter your decisions through, you are building an internal habit of prioritizing your decisions based on what is most important to you.

There are two primary types of values. The first is moral values. These are the basic values engrained in our culture and, in many cases, our DNA. They could be principles such as honesty, fidelity, integrity, hard work, etc. While these values are important, they are not the type of values I am referring to when I talk about core personal values. Core personal values are preferential values. They are the individual values that make you unique, spark your passion, filter your decisions, and guide your path. While these must be aligned to your moral values, they are not necessarily the same. They are unique to you.

Also, for many, values have become more like aspirational intentions, meaning that they are simply something we hope to live up to, rather than actual values that are used to filter and guide decisions. If your life does not consistently line up to them, then they are not really core values. Every decision requires you to weigh the pros and cons of the decision. If it is truly a core value, your choices will consistently line up with it.

Finally, our values have deeper meaning. For that reason, it is important to define what that value means for you. We may both have the same core value, but they can mean very different things.

Core Value Example: Advocacy

Core values come from such a deep place within us that we ought to be able to see their influence in pretty much everything we do. For that reason, it is my hope and expectation that you see evidence of my core personal values as you read this book. To help you see how this works, I'll share what my core values are, then explain one of them. My core values are faith, authenticity, wonder, advocacy, and impact.

Now, let's take a deeper look at what it means to me to have a core value of advocacy. It means that I actively seek ways to bring out the best (the gold) in others. I look for ways to make my ceiling their floor and then work to accomplish that. I actively help others understand their identity, believe in themselves more, and practically live as who they are created to be. I am a champion for others as they overcome challenging life circumstances, and I will stand up for others when they are not present.

Being able to articulate what advocacy means in my life helps me gauge whether I am actually living it. Also, it can help clarify how I, with my value for advocacy, might look or behave differently from someone else who also has the same core value. For example, my living this value as a business consultant probably looks quite different from how a social worker or attorney would live it, though someone working in those fields could easily have advocacy as one of their core values.

More practically speaking, then, what does it look like for me to live out advocacy in my life right now? To name a few, I am developing *Unstoppable* to provide a simple platform, tools, resources, and support for people to step into who they are created to be. I regularly take time to coach people. I recognize that I need to do a better job of first seeing the gold, before seeing negatives, in my kids and my team. I also recognize that I sometimes need to do a better job of being an advocate for myself.

You can see from this example how articulating your core values will help you be more intentional about focusing your energy on what is truly most important to you, while also showing areas of your life that are not fully in alignment with your values. Those areas are likely places where you are already experiencing some level of conflict or friction, and bringing them into alignment with your core values will help alleviate that stress.

ASSESS: Where Are You At?

Take a moment to reflect on your core values. Have you identified core personal values for your own life? If so, how are you filtering all of your decisions through them? How are you intentionally living them each day? If the circumstances of your life were to significantly change, would those values still be core to you?

If you haven't identified your core personal values, think about what happens when the challenges of life hit you. What foundation do you grab onto to make it through those difficult times? What if you had core values that could help guide your decisions?

Finally, pay attention to the emotions that rise up. Note them as clues to reflect on further as you go through this journey.

ALIGN: Keys for Success

By now, you may have some ideas about what words you could choose to articulate your core values, but before you start to pick these values, here are a few guidelines you will want to remember.

Like your mission, core values are timeless and can be applied in any circumstance. For example, when Rob died, my circumstances (and the vision for my life) completely changed. I thought I would be married forever. Yet I suddenly found myself middle-aged, widowed, and the sole parent to four kids. However, my mission and core values stayed the same. In fact, by having them I was able to find my anchor in one of the greatest storms of my life. As I faced many decisions, too many options, and an uncharted future, I was able to lean on my mission and core values to help me determine which direction to go.

If you find something that is important to you, but it only applies in certain circumstances, then it is not a core value. Keep digging to find the three to five values that truly guide your decisions regardless of time or circumstance. Similarly, if you find yourself saying, "I should ..." about any potential core value, then it is not a core value to you. True core values say, "I must ..."

Finally, remember that you are not trying to define good attributes or ways of living. Moral values are, of course, vitally important, but they are different from our core values. Consider my list again: faith, authenticity, wonder, advocacy, and impact. Notice that moral values like honesty, fidelity, or integrity could be behaviors my core values would manifest as they are lived out, but none of them would be considered a moral value.

APPLY: Key Questions and Activation

The easiest way to discover your top three to five core values is to start with options. You can use values tools, like the Unstoppable values cards that we have available at www.wearetheunstoppable. com, to help you limit the options. However, if you do not have these kind of cards, there are lists of core values online. Or you can simply list out the words that come to mind as you think about what is important to you.

Once you have a list, begin to sort through it. (Remember, these are not the only words that could represent your values. This is simply a way to get you started.) Select values that resonate with you. Pay attention to your intuition; some feel this in their heart, while others feel it in their gut. If you find yourself feeling it in your mind (thinking or "brain hurting"), then you are outside your intuition and may be overthinking. If you are struggling to identify values, eliminate the ones you know are anti-values.

Once you narrow down the list to your top three to five core values, the following steps will help maximize the benefit they give you. Again, you don't have to do this all at once, and you don't have to answer all these questions. However, the more that you do, the more benefit you will gain.

- Write down your values.
- Write down any phrases or examples of what these values mean to you.
- What are the three to five unique values that are the filter through which you view your life?
- Why did you choose the values you did? In other words, why are these values important to you?
- How do your values guide your decisions now and in the future?
- After working through the questions, fill out the following template for each of your core values:

I value _____, which to me means _____ (define in your own words) because _____ _____ (why it matters to you).

At first, I recommend writing two to three statements that describe each value statement and carry them with you. That will help you remember them when you need to make critical decisions. For example, here are the statements for my value of faith:

- I have faith in things I can't see.
- I am willing to risk even when I am scared or unsure.
- I seek hope when I feel like there is none.
- I don't rely on my own strengths.
- I draw on my past testimonies, make declarations, and seek others who have been where I want to go.

Eventually, these will become a subconscious part of who you are and you will automatically remember them.

Vision

The key questions you want your vision to answer are: How far out can you reasonably look on the path toward fulfilling your mission? What specific target can you see that will help you know you are on the right path?

Your vision is the focus you put on accomplishing your mission. A clear vision helps you create plans, set goals and objectives, make decisions, and coordinate the work you need to accomplish in order to achieve your mission. A vision helps keep individuals or organizations focused and together, especially with complex projects and in stressful times. It also provides a way to create energy and momentum as you set out to accomplish your mission in life. Unlike your mission and values, your vision *does* change based on your circumstances. It becomes your GPS for finding the best way to get to your target destination.

A vision helps you focus and clearly see a desired future state. A vision is your *what*—what you envision for your future. While your mission is internal (intrinsic), the vision is external (extrinsic). It gives you and others a clear picture of what you are aspiring to accomplish. A vision sets things in motion.

For the last twenty-five years, I have gone away in January

to reflect on my mission and values and write a new vision for the upcoming year. I start by writing down my top one hundred dreams for the year and then narrow them down to the top twenty-five dreams based on the primary focuses of my life: health, faith, relationships, finances, and professional development. Then I create a vision board for the year. This vision board helps me focus on what I'm going after that year. I go through this same process with my team. It is amazing how that process sets things in motion for the rest of the year, even during the times when life gets busy and I don't revisit my vision often.

Make It SMART

By default, any target will be a certain distance from the person aiming at it. In the same way, before working to articulate your vision, decide what horizon is most comfortable for you as an individual or group. Is it one year, five years, fifty years, or something else? I chose a one-year horizon because of all the uncertainty and change I had been experiencing in my personal and professional life over the last couple of years.

Included in what I just said about my personal vision is another important piece. I assessed my life to see what was reasonable for me in this season. That meant setting a one-year horizon for my vision, but maybe you have more stability, so you could reasonably look further ahead than that. Or maybe looking a year out feels uncertain to you and you need to set your horizon even sooner, like in the three-to-six-month range. Whatever you choose, make it reasonable so it is something you can actually attain. It is better to set it shorter term and experience success than to plan something more grandiose and fall short.

A good way to remember the attributes of a good vision is to make it SMART (Specific, Measurable, Attainable, Relevant to who you are, and Timely). Being *specific* makes your vision compelling and helps you know when you reach it. *Measurable* means that words like *more, better,* or *less than* are usually too imprecise. You need to use words that hold you accountable and enable you to celebrate victories. *Attainable* simply means keeping your vision realistic. *Relevant to who you are* means setting a vision that applies to you. And *timely* means defining an end date for the length of time you will be working to accomplish your vision.

Vision for Multiple Areas of Life

I recommend setting an overall vision for your life and then also setting smaller visions for different segments of your life. For example, I have vision statements written for my life in the areas of health and wellness, relationships (significant other, family, other relationships), faith or spirituality, personal development, financial, and professional. There can be more than one vision statement for each segment. For example, under the health and wellness area, I have three vision statements:

- By the end of 2019, I will have lost a total of a hundred and fifty pounds, will be measurably leaner and more fit, and will be healthier than when I was thirty.
- By March 2019, I will be able to fit into the special dress I bought.
- By the end of 2019, I will have more energy and vitality than ever before.

The main thing is to get a clear picture of what you need to do to get where you want to go. Sometimes you can say that in just one sentence; other times it will take two or three.

Then, once you have written your vision statements, an extremely helpful practice is to create a vision board. This is a simple exercise, but it is so powerful. Just take your statements for the different segments of your life and search for pictures to represent them. Compile the pictures onto one page where you can see them all, then keep your vision board in a place where you access it regularly. For example, I keep mine on my phone and computer as well as in my journal. I know of others who tape a physical copy onto their bathroom mirror or place it on their dresser. The point is to keep the vision in front of you, motivating you every day to keep pursuing what is most important.

ASSESS: Where Are You At?

Take a moment to reflect on your vision. Have you taken the time to dream and write those dreams down? Do you have a clear focus of what you want to accomplish in your life over the next few months? Year? Several years? Can you clearly articulate how your dreams may be realized over the next year? If so, how are you intentionally living your vision each day? If the circumstances of your life were to significantly change, what parts of your vision need to remain?

If you haven't identified your vision, think about what happens when the challenges of life hit you. What foundation do you grab onto to make it through those difficult times? What if you had a vision that could help guide your decisions? Finally, pay attention to the emotions that rise up. Note them as clues to reflect on further as you go through this journey.

ALIGN: Keys for Success

You are about to begin crafting your vision statements. As you do, here are a few reminders to ensure these vision statements will be most helpful to you:

Establish a horizon that inspires and stretches you yet is not overwhelming and unachievable, whether that's one year or fifty years. Again, I typically recommend starting with a shorter vision, like one year, until you feel comfortable with walking out vision in your life.

Remember that a clear vision will be SMART (Specific, Measurable, Attainable, Relevant to who you are, and Timely). Check for inspiration. A good vision statement will inspire you to dream beyond what you can do on your own. Then check for clarity. Do you (and any others involved) have a clear picture of what you are going after? Finally, check for alignment to your mission. All visions must lead you toward your mission.

Once you have your vision statements written down, create a vision board and declare your visions aloud. Doing all of this will start to rewire your brain to believe your vision is possible.

APPLY: Key Questions & Activation

You have done a lot of good work while going through this chapter. Remember that while this may stretch you because this kind of work is new, it should also be life-giving. As well, keep in mind that all these steps and questions will likely be helpful for you at some point, but they may not all be right now. Do as much as you can, but only what keeps you moving forward. And of course, enjoy the process!

Now it's time to write your vision statements. First, decide what horizon is most comfortable for you as an individual or as a group. Is it one year? Five years? Fifty years? Next, answer the following questions to form the elements of an overall vision statement for this next year:

- What do I want to accomplish?
- How will I know I'm on my way to accomplishing it?
- Can I realistically see myself achieving it?
- How is it relevant to what I want to accomplish in life?
- By when do I want it accomplished?

Take your answers to those questions and use or adapt this template to form your overall vision statement:

My overall vision for the next _____(time frame) is to _____ (what you want to accomplish) by _____ (when you want to accomplish it).

Now close your eyes and imagine what you see at the end of that horizon. Use your senses—what do you see, hear, feel, and smell? What are the outcomes you imagine? Who is there? Who is not there? What are you/they doing, or not doing? What is happening/not happening?

You may find it helpful to categorize your vision into key segments of life, as described earlier. I previously mentioned health and wellness, relationships, faith or spirituality, finances, personal development, and professional, but don't limit yourself to these categories. Rather, think of how you already segment your life.

Put together a vision board to visually represent your vision. Keep this vision board in a place where you can access it regularly, like on your phone or computer, in your journal, or anywhere else you will see it often.

Write out SMART vision statements for each of your life segments.

Declare your vision as you begin moving toward it. Also, as you move forward, try to act as if your vision is a reality. As your behavior begins to line up with your vision, it will become increasingly more real until it is eventually fulfilled.

Continue taking steps forward by testing and adding to your vision. Ask yourself, based on your passions and dreams, what you envision for your future. How is your vision big enough that it inspires and stretches you, yet is also achievable and not overwhelming? How is your vision aligned with your mission and values?

APPLY: Your Mission, Core Values, and Vision

Integrating Your Mission

If you have not articulated your mission before, living your mission will be new, which means developing new habits. These two final points are designed to help you do just that.

- What are one to three key takeaways from this section that you need to share with somebody else? Teach at least one other person to discover their mission.
- Keep testing, adapting, and sharing your mission until you feel energy rise up as you live it, speak about it, and teach others how to identify their own missions.

Testing Your Values

Test your values as you make decisions over the next several weeks. What are some ways that your values have shown up? What are some ways they are not showing up? What are some decisions you said yes to because they filtered through your values? What are some decisions you had to say no to because they did not fit your values? Share your values with others, and ask how they see you living those values on a daily basis.

- What are one to three key takeaways from this section that you need to share with somebody else? Teach at least one other person how to identify their core values to deepen the impact this will have for you.

Sharing Your Vision

Just as you did with your mission and core values, share your vision with others. Have them ask questions to further refine and focus your vision. Share your vision board with others.

- What are one to three key takeaways from this section that you need to share with somebody else? Teach at least one other person how to identify their vision, and encourage and show at least one other person how to create a vision board for their life. (Note: This is a fun exercise to do with family.)

Going Deeper

The steps you have taken so far in this chapter are huge, and you should celebrate what you have accomplished. Defining and living your mission, values, and vision is a layered process, not a destination. Below are some ways that you can go deeper in your discovery of your unique mission, values, and vision:

- Go to www.wearetheunstoppable.com to find simple and practical tools, such as our Legacy Discovery Journal and Unstoppable values cards that can help you define your mission, values, and visions.
- Register for online courses on defining your mission, values, and vision.

Chapter 4

PRINCIPLES

What Mindsets Need to Change?

have struggled with my weight my entire life. Until recently, I
was obese (except for a period during my teens where I was
severely anorexic and bulimic). On both sides of my family the
women have struggled with being overweight, so I had determined that I was genetically wired to be obese. I believe this
defeatist thinking hindered me from even attempting weight loss
over the years.

Can you relate to this? Do you have something in your life
that you have neglected to try because it has always been that
way, even through past generations? Maybe it was having no one
in your family go to college? Or coming from a family where
marriages never worked out? Often, we allow our beliefs about
the past to color how we approach the change we desire. However, the reality is that our beliefs can be made up of collections of
skewed realities based on past experiences, even the experiences
of past generations.

When I started down the path of losing one hundred and
fifty pounds, I had genetic testing done. I was shocked when the

results showed that I am actually not genetically wired for obesity. I also learned that I am genetically wired for diabetes. So all these years I believed the lie that I was meant to be obese when, in reality, I just needed to control my blood sugar.

Up to this point, we have been talking about establishing a strong foundation of who we are that will guide us toward our desired destination. However, most often the thing that prevents us from realizing our potential is our mindset, which is how we think about something. Changing our mindset is the primary key to getting unstuck. If we don't understand where we're stuck, we don't change the right things. By proactively identifying and changing how we think, we have the power to change how we act, react, and realize high performance.

It is important to note that our thoughts are not who we are. Rather, they are simply how we think. We cannot change who we are, but we have full control over how we think. So, considering that how we think controls how we behave, what we focus on, how we feel, the strengths we develop, and the timing within which we do things—which are all key parts of change—it would make sense that one of the most important things we can focus on when seeking transformation in any area of life is to start with understanding and changing how we think. Too often people avoid this critical step because they too quickly attach their thinking, behaviors, actions, and emotions to who they are. Then shame rises up and keeps their skewed ways of thinking locked up deep inside. When you take your thoughts captive, you have suddenly unlocked the power to change.

The key questions you will want to answer in this chapter are: What mindsets do I have that need to change around people, process, and governance? What mindsets need to change around who I am, my roles, and my future? What am I going to do to recognize and change blind spots, limiting beliefs, and strongholds?

Body: The Powerful Brain

Our brain is an amazing organ. It is no wonder that it is the central processing unit of our entire body. It is made up of over one hundred billion nerve cells that contain our thoughts and memories that branch off into "thought trees" mirroring to the left (focused on details that form the big picture) and the right (focused on the big pictures that lead to the details), working in synergistic harmony.[1] At any given time, we are receiving information from our five senses, building connections between that momentary experience and our stored memories in order to make sense of the new information, and then confirming or denying that information based on our interpretation of reality.[2] Our brain is the central function for our entire body, and it is the foundation for getting us unstuck, reversing limiting beliefs, and making and sustaining big change.

Mind: What Are Mindsets?

Unlike our brain, which is a central part of who we are, our mindsets are made up of a collection of twelve thousand to fifteen thousand thoughts that we have each day. A majority of these thoughts are subconscious, automatic, and habitual, and are based on the value judgments that that we make based on our past and current experiences.[3] Through these constant connections, our mindset is formed. This is the place where our thoughts are aligned to information and emotion, and our

---

1   Leaf, *The Gift in You*, 31.
2   Ibid., 68.
3   Peter D. Demarest and Harvey J. Schoof, *Answering the Central Question: How Science Reveals the Keys to Success in Life, Love, and Leadership* (Philadelphia: HeartLEAD Publishing, 2011), 25.

attitudes, perceptions of reality, and view of the world and ourselves (worldview and self-view) are formed.[4]

As we encounter new experiences, our emotions and other parts of our brain are at work to tell us whether we are safe and whether this experience lines up with our core values. If it lines up with our core values, we will embrace the experience. If not, we will reject it. Based on our perceived reality, our actions and behaviors will respond based on our natural and adapted behavioral tendencies. Repeating these experiences strengthens our newly formed brain patterns and develops our skills like the building of muscles.

The beauty of this is that, unlike our brain, our mindset is not who we are. Rather, it is simply how we think based on our perceived reality. Therefore, we have the power to bring these subconscious, automatic interpretations of reality up to our conscious level at any given time. When we bring subconscious beliefs into our conscious reality, we have tapped into the power to see clearly, get unstuck, reverse limiting beliefs, and change.

This is reflected in a quote I love: "Watch your thoughts, for they become words. Watch your words, for they become actions. Watch your actions, for they become habits. Watch your habits, for they become character. Watch your character, for it becomes your destiny."[5]

Do you consider yourself a glass-half-full or a glass-half-empty kind of person? The lens you look through will determine how you see the world and yourself. Why is this important for sustainable change? Because when you face a difficult situation with a glass-half-full attitude, you will dilate your heart and

---

4   Leaf, *Think, Learn, Succeed*, 37.
5   "Watch Your Thoughts; They Become Your Words; Watch Your Words; They Become Your Actions," *QuoteInvestigator*, https://quoteinvestigator.com/2013/01/10/watch-your-thoughts/.

increase the blood flow and oxygen flowing to your brain. This, in turn, will increase your clarity and ability to not only face the challenge, but also overcome it.[6]

Neuroscience (the study of the brain) has confirmed that how we think becomes a physical reality in our brain and body, affecting our optimal physical and mental health. Additionally, this science shows that it is our attitudes (the beliefs that form from our thought patterns) that determine our quality of life, not our DNA.[7]

In contrast to positive thought, negative or toxic thinking (glass-half-empty) has been proven to lead to negative physical consequences (cardiovascular and digestive problems, immune system disorders, and skin disorders), learning challenges, anxiety disorders (phobias, obsessive-compulsive behaviors, post-traumatic stress disorders, and panic attacks), depression, and a variety of addictions.[8] Since we have the power to choose to see our situation through either lens, why not be intentional about choosing to look at the situation through a glass-half-full mindset?

What a gift to know that my DNA is not in control of me! Rather, I get to choose to see myself as a healthy, fit individual who isn't sentenced to a lifetime of being obese. That realization has unlocked me from generations of limiting beliefs around my health, and it was the catalyst I needed to be able to lose over one hundred pounds in less than a year.

---

6 Leaf, *Think, Learn, Succeed*, 95.
7 Leaf, *Switch On Your Brain*, 13–14.
8 Leaf, *The Gift in You*, 174.

Growth Mindset versus Fixed Mindset

The way we continue to recognize and reverse the lies and limiting beliefs that keep us locked up is to develop a growth mindset, rather than a fixed mindset. Our brain is continuously changing, learning, unlearning, and growing. We have the power to harness this change and direct it toward the mission, vision, and desired changes in our lives.

In fact, newly emerging brain science called neuroplasty has proven that our brain has the ability to reorganize itself and physically change as we think, which has tremendous power to break off generations of toxic thought and negative thinking patterns. For example, if part of our brain is damaged, another part can take over some of its functions. The brain compensates for the damage.[9] So, in essence, we are wired for positivity and growth; therefore, we are wired for change. And you have the power to change.

Your mindset is simply a set of beliefs that frame a picture (or story) of what is going on based on how you perceive your circumstances, and it can be altered based on how you interpret their realities.[10] The fixed mindset creates a story that is focused on judgment: *This means I am a loser. This means I am powerless. This means they are out to get me.*

The growth mindset, on the other hand, focuses on learning, improvement, and partnering with possibility. It creates a very different story: *This means I have infinite value, regardless of circumstance. This means I am powerful, regardless of circumstance. What if they aren't out to get me? How would I perceive things differently?*

---

9 Ibid., 21.
10 *Mindset*, 215.

Since our brain is wired for positive thought, and we have the power to consciously control our thoughts, the simplest and fastest way to change is by proactively rewiring our brain. In fact, studies show that a positive environment and proactive thinking (bringing our subconscious thought into our conscious reality) can lead to significant structural changes in our brain in as little as four days.[11]

Proactively Rewiring Your Brain

Since proactively rewiring your brain is such a fundamental part of making big change simple, are you ready to get started? This process starts with synaptic pruning, which is the process of rewiring your brain to eliminate old thought patterns and create new positive thoughts, habits, and strengths. If you have the thought that you can't do something, you are able to rewire your brain to look through the lens of a different perspective to change that thought. By intentionally shifting your mindset, you disconnect your thoughts from old habits and the circumstances that support them. This process never stops, even when you are sleeping.

For example, I was trying to lose weight, but in the past I had the belief that I needed to eat every two or three hours or else my diabetes would drop my blood sugar too low. Therefore, I would be hungry every two or three hours. When I tried to go longer, I would ruminate on food. This led to a deeper belief system that I was never going to be healthy because my circumstance was that I had diabetes. Woe is me!

It wasn't until I changed my perspective and stopped giving influence to the circumstance of diabetes and the habit of

---

11 Leaf, *Think, Learn, Succeed*, 58.

eating every two hours that I was able to tap into the power of my strengths. By looking through the perspective that our bodies respond to sugar and that any protein or carbohydrate I eat produces sugar, which in turn spikes (and eventually crashes) my blood sugar, I was able to disconnect from the subconscious belief that I had to eat every two hours and reconnect to the conscious belief that I could control the amount of sugar I put into my system.

This conscious synaptic pruning allowed me to tap into the strengths of what I can control and eliminate the weaknesses of what I can't. Within a matter of days, my body was no longer craving sugar and my blood sugar had stabilized. Within a matter of weeks, I was eating one meal per day (habit). Within a matter of months, my diabetes had completely reversed (circumstance)! I could have pushed through and just started eating one meal per day, but it wouldn't have been sustainable. I needed to change my perspective (mindset) first, in order to create sustainable change.

The challenge is that as we change, our old beliefs aren't automatically removed. Rather, our new beliefs live alongside the old ones. As the new beliefs become stronger, they start to change and reinforce how we think, feel, and act.[12]

Our beliefs can either limit what we can do or help us develop abilities beyond our wildest dreams. When we choose a mindset that extends our current abilities, we experience greater satisfaction, emotional control, and mental and physical health.[13] However, if our brain interprets our circumstances as negative, dangerous, wrong, or unknown, it triggers a fight-or-flight response that causes us to avoid or resist change.[14] Therefore, in

12 *Mindset*, 214.
13 Leaf, *Think, Learn, Succeed*, 34.
14 Cloud, *Necessary Endings*, 38.

order to sustainably change, it is important to identify our negative and limiting beliefs and intentionally and proactively turn them positive. This starts with understanding the reality that guides our beliefs.

What Is Your Reality?

The first step to taking control of your thoughts is to uncover the subjective, skewed, and false realities (lies) that are tied to your past experiences. These are the realities that live in your subconscious mind and form the blind spots, limiting beliefs, and strongholds that keep you stuck.

When you look at this picture, what is the first thing you see? The gold goblet? The two people with hats, one of whom is playing guitar? An old man and woman staring at each other? The woman in the doorway? Do you see all or part of all those images?

Upon first glance, most people will see only one or two of the images. Few will see the entire picture. Some will even have such a strong attachment to one of the images that it is extremely difficult for them to see the others even when they are made aware of them.

This picture represents how we see the world and ourselves. Because of the stories that are living in our subconscious mind, our brains form thinking patterns that cause us to see only part of the picture. The objective reality (truth) of the picture is that there is a goblet, old man and woman, woman in a doorway, and two people sitting, but depending on the thought patterns that were formed from our past experiences, we have a tendency to see only part of the full picture. This becomes our subjective, or perceived, reality. Without knowing it, we could be believing and basing our decisions and actions on the lies of our perceived realities.

The first step to taking your thoughts captive is to look for the whole picture. It takes a growth mindset to do this.

Seeing the Whole Picture: Axiogenics

All our choices are determined by what we believe is the best or right thing to do in the moment, based on our perceptions. The challenge is that our perception of what is best, right, or true is often inaccurate. That is what was happening when you first looked at the picture above. Your mind decided what was valuable to see, and that is what your eye saw as reality. Because of this, it is important to approach any conflict or change with the assumption that you are only seeing part of the picture.

Our ability to make good and accurate value judgments is critical, because this cycle of perception, judgment, and meaning influences how we clearly see (perceive) situations and the biases we form (how we perceive the situation), and drives our priorities and decisions (how we think, how we act, our coachability, and our relative competencies). Looking for the whole picture is the most powerful part of change, because it actually changes your genetic expression and restructures your brain. The best news is that you are the only one who has control over this through the choices you make.[15]

Axiogenics is the science behind improving how we think. It is also the science of value, which measures our capacity to conceive and perceive value in ourselves, others, and the world, which then governs our subjective perspective. It answers the questions regarding value, values, goodness, morality, and ethics that guide all our subconscious and conscious decision making. We all have a personal-value hierarchy that tells us what is good versus bad related to ourselves, others, and the situations around us. The relative goodness of something is ultimately determined by its attributes and ability to fulfill its intended purpose.

For example, a car would have little value if it couldn't get us to where we wanted it to go, didn't have the features we valued, or didn't accomplish the purpose we have for it. This internal measure of good versus bad guides how clearly we see the situation, how we prioritize it based on other values, whether we interpret it as good or bad based on past experiences, and the ability and inner confidence we have to engage the situation.

It literally is the foundation and filter for all our choices, actions, and reactions, both good and bad. However, these definitions are often formed based on our skewed or partial realities, much like the picture above. The relative value of things is objective in nature (the whole picture), but our perception (the partial picture) causes us to place more or less value on something, which limits our ability to see the full picture, engage in the areas we don't see, or apply skills that come from that area. We are limiting our potential and don't even know it.

Have you heard the phrase "hindsight is 20/20"? This is actually not true, because our past experiences are not a clear picture

---

15 Leaf, *The Gift in You*, 28.

of reality, yet our brain relies on our experiences to form value judgments that guide current and future actions.

What if you could improve your ability to recognize the difference between skewed versus actual reality? Good versus bad choices? Your strengths versus your weaknesses? What if you could have 20/20 vision today and into the future? With axiogenics, you have the power to look through an objective lens and see the whole picture. By understanding and measuring your value hierarchy, you can recognize the areas of your subjective perspective that are skewed and intentionally reverse them in order to see from a more objective perspective. You are literally able to rewire your thinking in a way that will bring out your potential.

Remember, based on Maslow's hierarchy of needs, we are wired to realize our potential and to walk beside others as they realize their potential. We are not fulfilled in life until we do. Therefore, axiogenics is the way to take control of our mind in order to reach fulfillment in life.

Axiogenics helps us to see how we form thoughts, make decisions, and develop skills based on our worldview (people, process, and systems) and self-view (individuality, roles, future/ ideal self). These are each different parts of the whole picture.

Look around the room. What do you see first? If you see the people first, you likely have an intrinsic perspective (people or individuality) that guides your belief systems. With this belief system, you may tend to recognize the needs of people first, have strong empathy, or good communication skills.

If you saw what was out of order, what needed to get done, or what problem needed to be solved, you likely have an extrinsic perspective (process). With this belief system you would tend to recognize what is out of order, understand the best way to get from point A to point B most efficiently, and solve practical problems.

If you saw the norms or rules, authority, or were looking for systems or structures to guide you, you likely have a systemic perspective (system). With this belief system, you look for why things need to be done and value-reinforcing systems, structures, and authority.

Like only seeing part of the picture, if your belief systems only allow you to see part of these dimensions, you may miss out on the value that can come from the others. For example, if you overfocus on the system and rules, you may miss out on the needs of the people. Or, if you overfocus on the needs of the people, you may deliver what they think they want at the expense of what they really need.

The same is true with self-view. If you overfocus on the value or get your worth from the roles in life (work, parent, spouse, etc.), you may stay stuck because you don't place enough value on who you are outside of those roles. Or, if you overfocus on who you are becoming (hoping that the future is better than the present circumstances), you may not embrace or find meaning in your present season of life, which will prevent you from doing what you need to do to get to the future season.

As you can see, it can be surprisingly easy to create misperceptions in our brain between our thoughts, ideas, and actions. These misperceptions cause cognitive distortions, which are irrational patterns of thought and biases that shape how we see ourselves and the world around us and are directly linked to our emotions and feelings. Below are fifteen of the most common cognitive distortions that may be impacting your ability to see your situation clearly:

Intrinsic Distortions: (People and Individuality)

- Personalization: making everything about you or someone else
- Fallacy of control: being victim to other people or circumstances outside of your control
- Blaming: blaming self or others for emotional pain
- Emotional reasoning: allowing emotions to define truth
- Fallacy of change: the belief that people will change if enough pressure is applied (extrinsic motivation versus intrinsic motivation to change)
- Heaven's reward fallacy: the belief that self-sacrifice or self-deprecation will eventually be rewarded (false humility)

Extrinsic Distortions: (Process and Roles)

- Overgeneralization: deciding based on one single event or situation
- Jumping to conclusions: deciding without getting facts or clarifying
- Catastrophizing: magnifying the effect of things
- Fallacy of fairness: life isn't always fair and fair isn't always equal

Systemic Distortions: (Systems and Self Image)

- Filtering: only seeing the negative or positive (glass empty versus glass full)
- Black-and-white thinking: either/or versus both/and
- Global labeling (or mislabeling): applying an unhealthy universal label to self or others
- Always being right: the need to always be right (fear of failure)

- Shoulds: living through a life of rules (or expecting others to)

Without seeing and valuing the full picture, your potential is limited, your abilities are stifled, and you will lack the confidence and resilience necessary to sustainably change. Practically, this can be done by intentionally taking a step back and looking from a higher perspective. Ask yourself what you might not be seeing in the world around you or within yourself and seek feedback from others. Or, if you prefer a faster and more precise method, there are assessments based on the science of axiology that help you get there more quickly. You can access these assessments at our website, www.wearetheunstoppable.com.

Blind Spots, Limiting Beliefs, and Strongholds

Our ability to put the entire picture into focus, even when we have been made aware of it, can be further hindered by blind spots, limiting beliefs, and strongholds that have formed because of traumatic events, reinforced stories, lack of experience, or upbringing. Lack of clarity or too much focus on any one of these areas creates blind spots, limiting beliefs, and strongholds that prevent us from being able to see circumstances clearly, be coachable, and realize our potential. The good news is that we have complete control over our thoughts. Learning to recognize these is like the dashboard of a car. It points to potential red flags and problems that can prevent us from seeing our circumstances clearly.

Blind Spots

A blind spot, as you might imagine, is something we simply can't see. It could be because of lack of understanding related to the area we are focusing on, lack of experience, or lack of focus. In most cases, blind spots aren't intentional.

I started my first business when I was twenty-three. That business grew very quickly, and within eighteen months we had over thirty employees. I had gone to school for international business and focused on leadership, so I thought I had leadership figured out. However, through that process of growth, I quickly learned that I had no clue what it took to lead people.

When the tragic events of 9/11 were happening, I was frustrated because our employees wanted to watch the events unfold on television when we had deliverables that were due. I later realized that I had a significant blind spot that had been preventing me from seeing the individual needs of others. I didn't know any other reality than, "Get the work done!" Since then, I have spent my career working to understand and draw out the individuality of people. The work is just a byproduct of that. Had I not been able to see my blind spot, our business would have never been successful, and I wouldn't have found my calling and greatest gifts. My blind-spots were keeping me from being able to realize my potential.

Awareness and focus are what uncover blind spots so we can reverse them. Simple ways to uncover them are regularly asking others what they see in our life (especially those who know us well), looking around us to see what we might be missing, and understanding ourselves and others. We also use assessments to get to the root of these blind spots. After all, if we could easily see them, they wouldn't be blind!

Once you discover your blind spot, you can reverse it through awareness (bringing your subconscious thought into the conscious realm by thinking or reflecting on it), continuing to seek feedback, and embracing the healthy conflict we talked about in chapter 2.

Limiting Beliefs

Unlike blind spots that can't be seen, limiting beliefs tend to be limitations that we are aware of. They tend to form based on repeated instances of good or bad experiences that help us form our story around a circumstance, person, or ourselves.

For example, if a dog bit you in the past, your subconscious may have a tendency to form a limiting belief that all dogs are bad. With this limiting belief, the next time you meet a dog, you may assume that dog will bite you, and your fight-or-flight response may cause you to be fearful, avoid the dog, or protect yourself. Because our subconscious groups experiences, you might have that same guardedness or lack of trust rise up when you meet other animals or even other people. The reality is that not all dogs are bad, so this limiting belief causes you to see and react to only part of the picture, leading you to miss out on the benefits related to whatever it is that you are avoiding.

These limiting beliefs can be ever so slight. They are typically coachable or more easily changeable because you would be more open to the reality that not all dogs are bad. However, limiting beliefs can be strengthened and reinforced by strong emotions (positive and negative). For example, if you were traumatized by the dog bite, strong negative emotions of fear or anger might come up, making it very difficult for you to believe any other reality other than "all dogs are bad."

You can often recognize limiting beliefs on your own. Listen for the "I should..." "I can't..." "I won't..." and "I never..." statements that rise up within you. These are the beliefs that tend to be rooted in a false or skewed reality. Or think about the phrases or beliefs that you grew up with, such as, "Nobody in my family has ever amounted to anything," or "I have never been able to do that."

Another way to recognize limiting beliefs is to pay attention to the things that have suddenly become harder or look for where you are settling for good versus great. There is likely an underlying belief that has caused that shift in ability.

One of my greatest strengths has always been my ability to notice things that are out of order, to solve problems, to make decisions, and to get things done quickly. However, after Rob passed, I noticed that it was very difficult for me to do these things. Of course, my kids loved it because I was no longer noticing the things that were out of order in the house. I was bothered by the fact that one of my greatest strengths had suddenly become one of my greatest weaknesses, so I took one of our assessments to get to the root of what was going on.

Sure enough, I had formed a belief system that said, "Details are overwhelming, they need to be avoided, and you need to think harder before making decisions." This made sense because I suddenly was a widow, the sole parent to four active kids, with two businesses to care for. I had become overwhelmed with details, so my fight-or-flight kicked in and said, "Run as fast as you can from any details or decisions, because they are *bad*!"

The good news is that limiting beliefs can be easily reversed by staying open and coachable, viewing circumstances as a process and not a destination, and remembering that how we think is not who we are. My lack of being able to effectively see what was out of order and make decisions was not who I was; it was simply a thinking pattern that was formed in response to a traumatic event.

A very practical way to reverse our limiting beliefs is to declare the opposite truth to the lie we are believing. Our brains respond to our spoken voice. Therefore, simply looking in the mirror and stating the opposite of our belief until it doesn't feel awkward is often all it will take to reverse our thinking. I am happy to report that after only four weeks of awkwardly looking in the mirror every day and declaring, "I do see details. I am a good problem solver. I can make decisions in this season," that I started to hear from those close to me that something seemed to have shifted and "Michelle was back."

I had also noticed that making decisions or noticing things that were out of order didn't require as much energy (the kids weren't exactly happy with that!). So I retook the assessment. Sure enough, the area of my thinking related to recognizing detail and solving practical problems had gone back up.

Another simple tool is to practice using your nondominant hand for a period of time until you see your mindset shifting. This is especially helpful when you have stronger limiting beliefs that are keeping you stuck, as the exercise forces your brain to open up to a new way of doing things.

Strongholds

Unresolved limiting beliefs or extremely traumatic events may form hardened belief systems known as strongholds. These belief systems tend to be reinforced with stories and lies that make it more difficult to be open to possibilities or being coachable.

Several years ago, I had a traumatic experience that caused me to lose trust in people. It formed a subconscious stronghold that said, "People will hurt you, so don't let your guard down." Despite years of coaching, I couldn't reverse that stronghold. Because of my strong understanding of people, it would only show up when I was under stress, but it caused lots of problems in relating to people. I struggled to trust, delegate, and effectively communicate with others.

Because our subconscious can't always separate circumstances, this reared its ugly head again when Rob passed. His passing reinforced my story because my subconscious was screaming, "See, Michelle, Rob and God let you down! I have been telling you that you need to protect yourself for all these years." As a result, I found myself pulling back instead of drawing toward the very help that I needed in that season. But as I started to declare the opposite truth, that they did not let me down and that not all people will let me down, I was able to let others into my world, and my influence and leadership ability grew along with it.

Research shows that we tend to become emotionally attached to our own ideas and resistant to others' ideas in about 95 percent of all relationships.[16] Therefore, it will take a very strong voice in your life to help you reverse a stronghold. As mentioned earlier, the strongest voice we have is our own, so the best way to recognize and reverse a stronghold is to find the stubborn areas where it is difficult to declare the opposite. Like with limiting beliefs, these are the areas where you find yourself saying *never, no way, can't,* or *won't.* They are the areas where you can't possibly imagine another reality.

Another way to recognize your strongholds is to watch for when heightened emotions rise up. Not only will this help you get unstuck and reverse strongholds, but it is a critical part of your overall emotional and physical health.

Heightened Emotions

Our emotions are like the dashboard on a car. They provide indicators about our overall health and well-being, actual and perceived threats from our environment, and the places where we may have skewed or limiting belief systems. Love and fear are the root of all emotions, and the others (joy, passion, enthusiasm, optimism, hopefulness, contentment, frustration, overwhelm, worry, doubt, anger, hatred, jealousy, insecurity, etc.) grow from these.

---

16 Demarest and Schoof, *Answering the Central* Question, 28.

Scientists have discovered that love and fear cannot co-exist, so at any given moment your thoughts are either operating out of one or the other.[17] Also, fear is not a natural part of how we were created; it has been learned. We are actually wired for love (and its related emotions) but have learned to fear because of our response to our circumstances.[18] This learned fear is reinforced as we allow our unconscious thoughts to dominate our responses and trigger heightened emotions. Once our emotions are out of control, we completely block our ability to think, rationalize, and be objective.

Allowing heightened emotions (either positive or negative) to dominate our thoughts for too long causes stress. Science has proven that stress is the number one killer and is the basic cause for more than 60 percent of all human illness and diseases.[19] Additionally, prolonged stress has a significant negative impact on our health.

There are three primary types of stress—physical (actual stress on the body or environmental stressors caused by pollution, chemicals, food, etc.), cognitive or mental stress (caused by misperceptions), and emotional stress (caused by heightened emotions). Emotional and cognitive stress will likely lead to physical stress over time.

Some people believe that they work best under stress. However, the reality is that stress just compels us to do "something." However, the best we can do under stress is only as good as the best we have learned to be, because we are operating from a subconscious versus conscious place. Since our subconscious is

---

17 Leaf, *The Gift in You, 143.*
18 Ibid., 148.
19 American Medical Association, How stress affects the body. 2010. Infographic. Institute of HeartmathWeb. 3 Dec 2013. http://www.heartmath.com/infographics/how-stress-effects-the-body.html.

driven by past memories and emotions, it is likely far from our best. So while we might be getting a lot accomplished, it is likely a whole lot of nothing!

Some stress is good because it causes us to be alert and open to change, but too much stress produces chemicals in the brain that can cause significant health consequences like high blood pressure, inflammatory response, slowed healing, blood sugar imbalances (linked with weight gain and diabetes), increased risk of heart attack and stroke, suppressed thyroid function, and impaired cognitive ability, all of which limit our ability to sustainably change.

Stress is essentially the gap between our actual and perceived realities. It can be enhanced by various internal and external stressors. These stressors cause our amygdala (the subconscious fight-or-flight part of our brain) to become overactive and our neocortex (the logical part of our brain) to become underactive, preventing us from being able to apply logic, intelligence, or reasoning to our situation.

It is a result of an overresponse to a perceived threatening situation. Our amygdala doesn't know the difference between reality or subjective reality, so once it perceives a threat, it sets off a chain reaction of chemicals (cortisol, adrenaline, norepinephrine, and others) that alerts our body to the actual or perceived threat. These chemicals stimulate the amygdala and suppress the hippocampus (our gatekeeper of long-term memories), which causes us to experience the "brain freeze" phenomenon and shuts down our ability to remember details or make decisions. This causes us to overfocus or underfocus on what we believe is reality, rather than the actual reality in front of us.

The problem is that in our current world of high stress, fast pace, and constant change, our body is in a constant state of perceived threat. Our physical reactions are the same whether our threat is real or imagined, therefore there is enormous power in our ability to control our thoughts to recognize what is real and what is subjective reality.

While we can't control our perception of reality (subconscious thought), we can control our perspective (conscious thought). Therefore, stress is optional. We can, and need to, proactively bring our subconscious thoughts into conscious reality, recognizing the cognitive distortions that are causing us to see only part of the picture, and reverse heightened emotions that put us into a state of stress.

ASSESS: Where Are You At?

Think about the change you want to make.

- As you think about your change, where do you recognize yourself looking through a fixed mindset (judgment) versus a growth mindset (possibility)?
- Take a step back and look to see the whole picture. Do you see the needs of the people involved in your change? Do you see what is out of order, what needs to get done, or the best way to get it accomplished? Do you see why the change is important? Do you see the systems, structures, rules, and authority that need to be considered as you change?
- What cognitive distortions do you recognize that may be holding you back from seeing the full picture of your circumstances?
- What belief systems, mindsets, blind spots, limiting beliefs, or strongholds might be keeping you stuck?
- What heightened emotions rise up as you think about this change?

ALIGN: Keys for Success

Consciously taking your thoughts captive; identifying where you are missing the whole picture; reversing blind spots, limiting beliefs and strongholds; and normalizing heightened emotions will open you up to making and sustaining your desired change. However, it is a continual process of bringing your subconscious thoughts and habits into a conscious place. It takes consistent awareness and intentionality. Here are some tips to help you.

Reflection Time

How often do you just let your thoughts wander through your mind unchecked? Do you take the time to pause, think, and reflect on your thoughts, feelings, and emotions? Just taking a few minutes every day to think and reflect starts the rewiring process in your brain. In fact, learning to capture and evaluate your thoughts is one of the most significant ways take care of yourself mentally, be more self-aware, and regulate your emotions and behaviors.[20]

As you think, the actual physical nature of your brain changes and can remove toxic patterns and replace them with healthy thoughts, leading to increased intelligence and brain, mind, and physical health.[21] The more you think, the more brain connections you grow.

Think of reflection as taking your brain to the gym. This mental training increases the number of changed neurons that survive and the number of meaningful (positive reinforcing) memories that are stored in your brain, especially when your

---

20 Leaf, *Think, Learn, Succeed*, 51.
21 Leaf, *Switch On Your Brain*, 20.

desired change is particularly challenging.[22] As a result, taking time to reflect daily will literally create new habits without your even starting the work of building them. Many of us spend countless hours at the gym building our body strength, but we don't take time to build the most powerful thing for realizing sustainable change—our mental strength.

Positive Thoughts and Declarations

There is power in our words! You will see this theme repeated throughout this book. Our spoken word is one of the most powerful tools to use when attempting to get unstuck, make change, and unlock our potential.

We discussed earlier that our brains are wired for positivity. However, constant stress has created a learned fear response to our circumstances that keeps us blinded, stuck, and in a place of heightened emotion, limiting our ability to change. However, declaring the opposite, positive truth to any negative thought or emotion will literally reverse this learned fear and destroy the toxic memories in our brain.[23] Science shows that whatever we think about the most grows, so when we constantly worry or think about something negative, we shouldn't be surprised if we struggle with negative emotions or physical illnesses.

Our words are the outflow of our internal thoughts. Like our thoughts, they contain the power to literally change our brain and body structure. Often, we don't even realize the times that we unintentionally speak death over ourselves. I remember reading about a science experiment that proved this point. The researchers put two plants in the same controlled environment. They spoke only positive words over one and only negative words over

---

22 Leaf, *Think, Learn, Succeed*, 33.
23 Ibid, 61–63.

the other. In a very short time, the plant that had negative words spoken over it shriveled up and died, whereas the plant that had positive words spoken over it flourished.

Researchers have shown that negative and hurtful words affect the same part of our brain (the cingulate gyrus) as a physical injury. However, when we speak words of love and affirmation,

the brain releases oxytocin, which literally destroys the toxic thought clusters and rebuilds new nontoxic ones.[24]

One practical way to pay attention to our words is through negativity fasts. I regularly practice these fasts from negative words by paying attention to the number of times I speak negativity in a certain period of time. I have the kids (and others in my life) listen for them and hold me accountable. We have a code phrase—"the power of your words"—that they say to me when they hear me saying anything negative. It is amazing how many times I say things like, "It kills me..." "I can't..." "I shouldn't..." or "I hate..." All of those are words reinforce toxic thoughts and do not lead to life.

Accountability Partners

Our mind is the most powerful tool we have to get unstuck and make sustainable change. However, because our thoughts are formed from our experiences, we rarely see the whole picture. Additionally, our experiences and the experiences that have been passed down through the generations have formed thinking patterns, blind spots, limiting beliefs, and strongholds that keep us stuck. Therefore, it is critical to have people in our lives who can help us see the areas we don't see, help us see from different perspectives, and encourage us with positive reinforcement.

---

24 *The Gift in You*, 196.

Science shows that the more removed we are from human connection, the greater the chance is that we will view the world and ourselves through a skewed reality.[25] (We will talk more about building a support structure of accountability partners to help you sustain your change in chapter 7. However, since approaching your change with the right mindset is so critical, I felt that it was a key to success that shouldn't be missed here.)

APPLY: Key Questions & Activation

- What limiting mindsets may be at the root of your negative behaviors, which keep you from being your greatest self? (Ask someone close to you to help you identify any you might be missing.)
- What are three to five empowering declarations (that are the opposite of your limiting mindsets), which will help you believe what's possible so you can see growth in your life?
- Going forward, how can you recognize and change blind spots, limiting beliefs, and strongholds?
- What are one to three key takeaways from this chapter that you need to share with somebody else? Teach at least one other person about these takeaways.

Go to www.wearetheunstoppable.com to find simple and practical tools that can help you make and sustain your change.

- Download worksheets that will help you understand your cognitive distortions and uncover blind spots, limiting beliefs, and strongholds that might be keeping you stuck.

---

25 Leaf, *Think, Learn, Succeed,* 88.

- Take an assessment that will help you identify your current thinking patterns, blind spots, limiting beliefs, and strongholds.
- Register for online courses on shifting your mindset to drive the change you need.

Chapter 5

___

PRACTICES

What Do I Need to Do Differently?

When most people want to change something in their life, they start by trying to do something different, but fail to take time to build a strong foundation around what brings them passion, clearly define the change they want to make, set vision and boundaries that align to their purpose, and address mindsets (principles) that might be keeping them stuck. Then, when the desired change they were seeking doesn't materialize, they either get frustrated and quit or they find that they have gone down a wrong path and have lost the motivation to keep going when the going gets tough. Does any of this resonate with you?

In order to create new habits, you must first be able to perceive greater potential value in the new habit. That requires you to start with mindset. However, when you do the work that was laid out in chapters 1 through 4, the rest of the work is relatively easy.

Most of us would simply start doing activities, attempting to muscle our way into new habits. However, simply doing things differently won't help you make your change, let alone sustain it.

It requires an understanding of how we as humans harness passion, purpose, and mindset into new ways of doing things, as well as some simple keys to making sure we are engaging in the right activities, for the right reason, in the right manner.

I tried to lose weight my entire life. I understood the best practices around diet, exercise, and healthy living, but it wasn't until I had the right foundation in place (aligned to my mission of bringing out the gold in myself and others), focused my weight loss on a deeper *why* (being a healthy role model for my kids), and had reversed some key limiting beliefs (genetics, blood sugar, and the mindset that I couldn't eat certain foods) that I was truly ready to sustainably lose the weight. I would be lying if I said it didn't come without great sacrifice. However, losing one hundred pounds in the first year was—surprisingly—relatively easy.

This chapter focuses on what you need to do differently in order to accomplish your desired change. The key questions you'll want to answer are: What do I need to do differently? What are some best practices to learn from? How can I "act as if" in my current role?

What Should You Stop, Start, and Continue?

Change requires that we stop doing things that are preventing us from achieving our desired outcomes or are producing unhealthy conflict, and start or continue doing things that move us in the right direction and produce healthy conflict. However, it can be difficult to stop doing the things that have caused us to produce the same results in the past. Habits can be hard to break, so it is important to be intentional about reflecting on the things that need to come to an end.

Read that carefully: *things that need to come to an end.* That alone is an essential mindset for us to cultivate in pursuing the life we want. If we are unwilling to end what is good, we lose the ability to start what is best.

Our brains are hardwired to read the situations around us. If they interpret them as negative, our tendency is to either fight against it or avoid it. That's why it's so important to recognize the difference between the unhealthy conflict and healthy conflict that we talked about in chapter 3. Unhealthy conflict can come in many different forms, but some ways unhealthy conflict presents itself are as persistent stress, regularly feeling worn out emotionally or physically, or an inability to overcome a particular issue. Healthy conflict in this case looks like rejecting the well-worn paths that keep getting us where we don't want to go. It's uncomfortable, so it feels like conflict, but it is both healthy and necessary.

The ability to let go of things in your life is an important part of making sustainable change. It allows you to let go of what is bad, or even good, in order to be ready for what is great. Many times, we become trapped because we aren't willing or able to let go of old habits, ways, or activities in order to form new  ones. This can even include being willing to embrace something that maybe didn't work in the past.

One of the most common things that keeps my clients stuck and prevents them from trying new ways is that they have "tried it before." However, as you go through your change journey you will have different readiness, levels of maturity, mindsets, and opportunities that can make ways that didn't work previously be wildly successful today. Therefore, it is necessary to be willing to give up what you have done in the past, what did or didn't work, and even past successes, to be open and ready to build new habits that will get you to where you want to go.

This process is a pruning of sorts. Trees are pruned in order to get rid of dead, broken, or damaged branches; prevent damage from falling branches; provide the light that is necessary to promote growth; train the trees to grow on your terms; give them a polished look; and set the tree up with a good foundation for long-term growth. Much like with trees, pruning is an important part of making sustainable change. It requires letting go of what was, for a much better future.

Forming New Habits

Once you have let go of old ways, it is important to intentionally build a habit around the new ways that will help guide you to your desired outcomes. However, some habits are helpful while others are hurtful. It is important to make sure you have the right mindsets in place in order to build the right habits to support and reinforce positive change.

In chapter 4 we touched on the fact that whatever you think about the most will grow. Brain science proves that the more we focus on a repetitive thought, the stronger the new ways become, forming habits and permanent change. This is called attention density.[1] The more attention we give something, the denser the thought or action becomes.

There are three levels of thinking that reinforce our thoughts and actions. Level one is the thoughts that disappear within twenty-four to forty-eight hours. This is why we can wake up from a dream, have full recollection of it, and then forget it an hour later—or sit in a class but then the next day not remember most of what was talked about.

Level two involves the reflective thought that we discussed in

---

1   Demarest and Schoof, *Answering the Central Question*, 61.

chapter 4. However, if we stop feeding the memory by thinking about something new, we will forget most of it. Studying or practicing something at least seven times in repeated intervals over time is a simple and practical way to start to reinforce new habits (the first four days are the hardest). This is why many diet plans start with three- or four-day detox or fasting periods. Also, this is why we need to communicate something "seven different times, seven different ways" to ensure that a message is understood and received by a group of people.

Level three involves constant, deliberate, and intentional activity daily for at least twenty-one days. Perhaps you have heard the phrase "it takes twenty-one days to form a habit." This level of thinking builds strong connections and the protein changes needed to create a long-term and integrated memory.[2] In order to create automatic and unconscious habits, it takes about sixty-three days of repeatedly thinking about or acting on new ways.[3] And it takes about ninety days to reinforce and sustain our habit.

Without intentionally working to form new habits, our brain reverts to relying on our subconscious mind, since it can multitask and process more efficiently than our conscious mind. This causes programed mental habits to dominate our actions. Once our thoughts and actions have been repeated long enough, they become programmed into our brain as a set of neuropathways and connections, and live within our subconscious. Yes, you read that right, we are not wired to be able to effectively multitask *unless* we have created a habit that has been repeated long enough to become an automatic part of our subconscious.[4]

---

2 Leaf, *Switch On Your Brain*, 128.
3 Leaf, *Think, Learn, Succeed*, 216–217.
4 Demarest and Schoof, *Answering the Central Question*, 53.

Too often, we try to break old habits or create new ways of doing things through merely thinking positive thoughts, pushing through, or faking it until we make it, and then wonder why we run out of energy so quickly. However, this cultural approach to change rarely produces sustainable change. Eventually, the automatic old habits will resurface and dominate our behavior. We can tell we have created a lasting habit if we automatically do it without having to think about it, track it, or be held accountable to it.

Get Off Go

As we are creating new habits, thinking about everything we need to do differently can get overwhelming. As the new brain pathways are being developed to create new habits, the old ones are trying to fight off the change. The brain is literally fighting between its innate need to positively grow and the comfortable feeling of staying the same. When this happens, we tend to take on too much and then fail or not get started because of feeling overwhelmed. This makes it critical to just "get off go."

In his book *Blink*, Malcolm Gladwell makes a compelling case that snap decisions or judgments are often better than well-thought out introspective ones. He goes on to say that the best decision makers aren't those who process information or spend time deliberating. Rather, they are the ones who are able to filter through to the few things that matter amid an overwhelming number of variables.[5]

What Gladwell is talking about is the importance of instinctive decisions. When we make an instinctive decision, we are engaging that filtering mechanism rather than allowing our brain to

---

5   Malcolm Gladwell, *Blink: The Power of Thinking Without Thinking* (New York: Little, Brown and Company, 2005).

continue to filter through a countless number of considerations, possibilities, judgments, and assumptions that are likely skewed.

It is important to ask, "What *can* I do?" However, many times we set unrealistic expectations about what we can do. Remember the maturity model from chapter 3? We are all at various stages of our change journey. Therefore, planning to dive in and completely master the change is unrealistic and will cause unhealthy conflict that will prevent and kill your change rather than cause the healthy conflict that will foster your change.

So, it is important to assess where you are in the journey and meet yourself there. If this is a new change (infant), then what is one thing you can do to try out the new change? If you are revisiting a change you have started to make in the past with little success (toddler), what did work in the past? Maybe start there. If you have had some reasonable success with your change but are looking to take it to the next level (adolescent), seek out best practices for what the next focus could be. And if you have had consistent results in your change over time (adult), you may want to create new best practices that make you a benchmark for others.

Start to apply your change to other areas of life or begin walking beside others who are further behind you in your change. Don't just try to accomplish it all. Rather, identify the best place to start and "get off go." Like Nike says, Just Do It!

ASSESS: Where Are You At?

- Ask yourself these questions as you think about the change you want to make.
- What are some things you need to start doing, stop doing, or continue doing (reinforce) in order to successfully make your change?

- What old ways or habits are keeping you stuck or preventing you from achieving your goals? What ways have you tried (and failed) in the past, that you could revisit again?
- How have you intentionally built time into your day to reinforce level-three thinking and action?
- Despite what is keeping you stuck or preventing you from achieving your goals, what *can* you do to move toward your desired outcomes?
- What heightened emotions rise up as you think about what you need to do differently?

ALIGN: Keys for Success

"Act As If": The Power of Intention

Even as a child, I was surrounded by the concept of setting goals. I had a goal to get an A in my classes, a goal to graduate from college and get a job, many New Year's resolutions, and even the daily goal to accomplish my never-ending to-do list. You would expect that if someone has goals, they should accomplish more, but this isn't always true. While goals are important to drive change, I believe that we often overlook the power of intention. I like to call this "acting as if."

Goals, like New Year's resolutions, often fail. This is because goalsetting is focused on the model of causality, which states that "if I do X, then I will get Y." This model is essentially a brain model that relies on our memories, experiences, and logical processing to determine what, where, when, how, and why we accomplish our goals. It tells us how things will go and what is true, at least based on our current perception of reality.

In contrast, the power of intention is a mind model. Rather than showing what *appears to be* true, as goal setting does, intentionality shows what *needs to be true*, because it is objectively more valuable than the alternate. Research on this model suggests that our mind can apply predictive power to our circumstances.[6] In other words, if you can see yourself achieving something in your mind, that goes a long way toward being able to achieve it in reality.

This is how people accomplish things no one has ever done or thought possible; they envisioned themselves as able to do it first. Just consider the countless examples of broken world records, such as the first man who ever ran a four-minute mile. At the time it had been declared physically impossible, yet after he did it, many others did as well.

Researcher Daniel Dennett suggests four practical steps to being able to harness this predictive power (we have already addressed the first three in chapters 1 through 3):

- Decide that your mind has the potential to be rational (reasonable and sound) and that your change, regardless of the size or scope, is also rational.
- Determine what beliefs you need to accomplish your goal or change, and the meaning and purpose that change has in the world.
- Using similar considerations, determine the characteristics or attributes that are needed for your goal or change.
- Finally, based on the assumption that if you were to act on the above, your goal or desired change will be realized, start to do it ("act as if" if it is already true).

When I was a kid, I wanted to be the first female President of the United States. That could have seemed like a dream that is

---

6   Daniel C. Dennett, "Real Patterns," *The Journal of Philosophy*, Vol. 88, No. 1. (Jan., 1991), 27–51.

completely unrealistic, until I learned about the power of intentionality. Then I was able to look at that dream, believe I had the potential to accomplish it, unpack the attributes of that role (minority surrounded by the majority, first to do things, disruptor, leader of many, making national or global impact), and bring those attributes into my current reality. I started to "act as if" I were the first female President of the United States in my current role as a consultant, business owner, and citizen.

It changed everything! I was brought into situations and opportunities that required all those attributes, my company and I became known as thought leaders in industries that we were very new to, and I started to develop disruptive models for leading individual and collective change. By "acting as if," I was able to tap into the predictive power of intention.

Am I the first female President of the United States? No—but I am the first female leader to make meaningful change in a multitude of situations. You see, we often set a goal based on the only grid we have at the time. I didn't have another grid for being a minority leader, bringing systemic change to the world. However, had I set out with a goal to be the first female President of the United States, I would have probably failed miserably. Even so, by acting as if I were president in every role I have played in life, I have been given opportunities to lead and impact the world that are beyond my wildest dreams.

"Acting as if" daily allows you to focus on who you are in the moment, recognize and live out what matters to you, and increase your engagement and empowerment. Unlike simply setting goals, these intentions are limitless. Since they are about who you want to be and what you want to contribute, they are expansive. They will not only make you more productive but will also open your mind and heart to new things.

They will get you wondering, experiencing, and learning.

They will take you out of your head (brain)—what's not working, what you can/can't do—and focus you on possibility, gratitude, and joy. And, most importantly, they will focus you on the contribution you can make today. When you focus on a small change, it can result in big differences.

Best Practices: Benchmarking for Success

A benchmark is a test used to compare performance between multiple things, either against each other or against an accepted standard. When I turn companies around, I always start by looking for benchmarks or best practices within the industry to see what drives greater performance and value. Since companies owned by private equity firms typically have better performance, I determine what they are investing in, how they are growing companies within that industry, and what they are willing to pay more or less for as they are buying and selling companies. This valuable benchmark helps me to focus on the critical few activities that will drive the greatest performance in that specific industry or company.

If benchmarking leads directly to comparing ourselves with a standard, why would we do it? Doesn't that set us up for being discouraged when we see how badly we're falling short? Well, it could lead to those things, but if we set aside our insecurities, it can also become one of the fastest ways to grow and maintain growth, because benchmarking is a way of discovering what is the best performance being achieved.

- Benchmarking provides a model that allows you to focus on best practices and proven methods so you don't have to "recreate the wheel."

- In business, it allows you to outperform other organizations within your industry. It improves your efficiency by constantly improving your performance through new ideas and procedures you learn from other companies. Since everyone wants to be the best, benchmarking gives you a competitive advantage when dealing with your customers.
- "My ceiling is your floor" principle—you don't always have to be the first innovator; you can learn from whoever is leading right now.
- It fosters continuous improvement.
- It also fosters collaboration and cooperation with others.
- It holds you accountable for performance.

Benchmarking against best practices occurs for good reason. Over time, best practices emerge based on the experience of what actions led to successful outcomes. In other words, this isn't about setting an impossible standard we can't meet; it's about identifying the people or organizations who are doing the best at what we want to do, figuring out what or how they do things, and then learning from them.

How to Benchmark

The first step to benchmarking is to determine what you are trying to benchmark and why. Ask, "What are successful models, examples, or best practices that relate to the outcomes and change I desire?" Then look for reliable sources that have proven results.

For example, when I set out to lose one hundred and fifty pounds, I looked for groups of people who had lost at least one hundred pounds. It wouldn't have been as effective or reliable had I benchmarked against people who had lost twenty or thirty pounds, because the mindsets and actions needed to lose a large amount of weight are different from those required to lose a little.

The next step is to look for the critical few things that caused their success. Performance-management science has proven that new behavior is reinforced best when we have identified the antecedent, which is something that needs to come before a desired result. It can be anything we see, feel, hear, smell, or taste. These don't cause behavior, but they do motivate and persuade it.[7]

For example, when you see a high-voltage sign, you know to not touch the wire, because you will likely get shocked. As I set out to lose weight, I looked to those who had lost significant weight to better understand the benchmarks (antecedents and best practices) that would likely give me the best results, such as stabilizing my blood sugar through limiting processed foods, carbs, or protein, and eating good, healthy fat; intermittent fasting; eating the right foods for my genetic wiring; drinking plenty of water; and doing high-intensity interval training. These benchmarks allowed me to focus my efforts on the best activities that would give me the fastest and most sustainable desired results.

Finally, set up a system of regularly measuring your progress against the progress and results of your benchmark. A simple, practical way of doing this is through joining a group of people who are going after similar change, such as a support group, cohort, or peer group. We have found that our clients' best results come when they are involved in one of these. This is why all of our training programs include best practices as a foundational step to

---

7   Daniels and Daniels, *Performance Management*, 99, 113.

any change and have some element of one-on-one or peer coaching, cohort-style training, or support after the training is done.

Be careful not to limit yourself and your potential based on a benchmark. What worked for others may not work for you, so start out with what has worked for you in the past, then integrate the best practices and antecedents of others who have gone before you. Finally, remember the power of intention. Act as if you have accomplished your desired outcomes. How would you show up differently? What would you be doing differently?

Lean Startup

One of the biggest mistakes I see people making with change is to overcomplicate the process or try to get things right the first time. This results in overwhelm and frustration that leads to failure. I can relate to this challenge, as I would call myself a recovering perfectionist. It wasn't until I learned about lean process that I realized the incredible power in approaching change in layers or stages.

Many businesses have started using the Lean Startup methodology to avoid needing the heavy up-front investment that kills most innovation before it begins. That is exactly what we need as we work toward the changes we want to make in our lives.

This method has four key principles that help us eliminate uncertainty: untested hypotheses, the minimally viable product, pivoting, and agile development.

Eliminating Uncertainty

Have you ever set out to change without a plan, taking a just-do-it approach that pushes through without any form of planning or management? Or, alternatively, have you spent so much time planning that you never get off go? The Lean Startup approach creates order by testing against the vision, desired outcomes, and guardrails. It is about being able to embrace failure as an opportunity to learn, grow, revise, and continue to change. If you cannot be vulnerable, cannot embrace failure, and cannot adapt quickly, you run the risk of spending too much time, resources, and energy on the wrong things, which will ultimately lead to failure.

Tested Hypotheses

Our strategies and plans are simply a set of hypotheses or guesses. We presuppose that if we make this change, we will achieve our desired outcomes. For example, I started my weight-loss journey with the hypothesis that if I lowered my caloric intake, I would likely lose the weight I needed to lose. However, I quickly learned that this hypothesis wasn't true for my body. In fact, once I started to apply some of the best practices I learned, I actually ended up having to eat more calories to consistently lose weight. I realized that I had wasted time, money, and energy applying a calorie-reduction behavior that wasn't even the answer to my problem. Can you relate?

Too often, we begin long and arduous change plans with a set of untested hypotheses that end up being wrong. It is important to look at change as a set of hypotheses that need to be tested early on and often throughout our change journey. One way to get started with eliminating uncertainty is to ask, "What do I know, what can I do, and what is the best/worst thing that could happen?" Then look around to find those benchmarks that can help you identify the best set of assumptions to start with.

The Minimally Viable Product (MVP)

The second principle of Lean Startup is the minimally viable product (MVP) test. An MVP is the most basic version of whatever it is that we are trying to change. It could be a new idea, product, or company, but it could also be weight loss, an improved relationship, or a new job.

Too often, people will spend way too much time and resources trying to get things perfect before they start to change. When I used to try to lose weight, I would spend countless hours creating meal plans based on calorie restrictions, spending hundreds of dollars to replace my high-calorie food, and rigidly planning out my days only to be exhausted before I even got started. This was obviously doomed from the get-go.

The MVP principle tries to avoid this by asking, "What is the most basic change I can make to test my assumptions as I go?" For example, in my case, "What food do I have that helps me test my assumption?" or "What food can I buy for the next three days to see how I do?"

Practically, this could look like focusing on the top one to three things you need to change, the top three to five key accountabilities that are needed for a new role, or the critical value or few features that a customer might want to see in a product or service. The key is to focus and limit your variables. Based on your understanding of the customer (either you, your peers, or external customers), which variables would be the most important to test? Over time, this will reduce the failure rate of your change and will ensure that you are doing the right activities to create sustainable change.

Once you have identified the most basic elements of your idea, product, or change, you then need to get out there and test them. This testing is based on a "build, measure, and learn" feedback loop where you are constantly building assumptions; testing and measuring them against your passion (mission, vision, and values), purpose (desired outcomes and guardrails, and purpose for change), and principles (mindsets and belief systems); and then learning and adapting based on what is working, what isn't working, and what needs to change.

It is important to test your change with those most affected by the change. When I am coaching people through this process, I typically recommend that as soon as they have identified their critical few assumptions and have developed their MVP, they get out and test it with at least ten different stakeholders.

For example, we used this MVP principle while writing this book. I started the process of writing the book a year ago. However, rather than sitting down and writing, I started by pulling together the change principles that we had developed, taught, and lived for the past fifteen years. Then I started to blog on various topics to see what principles had the most impact on people. Another layer of testing came through various change support groups that we formed online and through teaching at lunch-and-learns, workshops, and webinars. Through this process of testing, we were able to develop the platform of tested tools and resources that are available today.

At the back of this book, you will find a link to a feedback form. If you give us feedback on how this book has impacted your life (what is working); what challenged you or was confusing (what isn't working); and the suggested changes, tools, and resources (what needs to change), we will send you a free copy of the next edition. This is an example of an MVP in action. Rather than waiting to get it perfect, we are taking you along on the journey of guiding our writing and development process.

As a recovering perfectionist, it has been hard to put imperfect things out there, but through diligently practicing this principle, I have learned so much that made this book so much more relevant and impactful than it would have been had I simply sat down to write the book without those layers. Often, it feels like that up-front work slows down our change process, when in reality it speeds it up because we are taking meaningful steps that lead to the right change.

Pivoting: Failing Forward

The third principle of Lean Startup thinking is pivoting. As you are testing your assumptions and MVP, you will learn what is working, what is not, and what needs to change. Chapter 6 talks more about the reason and benefits behind experiential learning, and chapter 8 talks about the importance of learning how to fail. However, I think it is important to mention these thoughts here, because many times we prevent ourselves from getting started with change because we aren't willing to admit failure and pivot how we are going about change.

Studies show that experiential learning allows us to learn more quickly, reinforces new behaviors and habits more effectively, and makes the change process extremely personal and relevant. You wouldn't expect your toddler to have it all figured out when he/she is first learning to walk. You would walk beside them as they navigate little steps, manage falls, and wobble through clunky starts and stops. Eventually they will walk without help, but definitely not in the beginning, so why would you expect yourself to have everything figured out before you engage in a new change? Therefore, it is critical that you are open to adapting your assumptions, plans, and activities along the way in order to achieve the change you are seeking.

Agile Development: Validated Learning

The final principle of Lean Startup is agile development, or validated learning. This is a proactive method for demonstrating progress, despite extreme uncertainty in many cases. It focuses on making small, incremental changes and learning along the way.

Think of it like peeling an onion, versus taking a big bite out of an apple. Once you learn to embrace validated learning, your development process will reduce significantly. When you focus on the critical few things that are needed or valued (either by you if you are changing personally, or by your customers if you are changing organizationally), you won't need to spend months waiting for a beta launch to change your direction. Instead, you can adapt your plans incrementally, inch by inch, minute by minute.

A practical way to do this is to break your change down into manageable steps. In previous chapters we have talked about the science behind reflection, our brain's wiring, and building new habits. Practically, for validated learning to be effective, this would look like 90- to 120-minute segments of learning, 2-week sprints, and 90-day focuses. The tools and resources necessary to support this learning could look like business/change model canvases, strategic roadmaps, meal plans, planners, or checklists. We will talk more about these in chapter 7.

Individual Ways of Doing Things: Behavioral and Learning Styles

Different people will be naturally drawn to different elements of this chapter. We all have unique ways of learning and behaving, and that is a good thing. What is important is that we have at least some understanding of our own individual wiring, because this wiring will impact how we go about change. Some people are driven by big, risky change, while others prefer slower, intentional, safe change. Some people are verbal processors who need to talk things out, while others are internal processors who need more reflection time. Additionally, some people need to surround themselves with others in order to maximize change, while others work best alone. The key is to learn your unique behavioral and learning style so you go about your change in a way that drives the most amount of performance and creates the least amount of stress.

DISC

One of the best tools to begin understanding our internal wiring, when it comes to learning and behavior, is called DISC. This is a widely used behavioral assessment tool that measures four behavioral styles: Dominance, Influence, Steadiness, and Compliance. It's fairly simple to explain each of these on their own, but each person carries their own unique blend of them all, usually with one or two dominant characteristics.

Since DISC is observable, it's easy to get clues about a person's primary behavioral styles through simple observation. This can be gauged from spoken words; nonverbal cues such as tone of voice or facial expressions; written communication; or the way a person walks, sits, and converses. However, using an assessment to gauge a person's true DISC profile is the most-effective way to quickly understand more about their behavior. In order to understand your individual behavioral (DISC) style, go to www.wearetheunstoppable.com.

Manage Your Energy, Not Your Time!

One of the top skills that the leaders I work with desire to grow is their time management. But time is finite while energy is infinite, so what if we were to focus on managing our energy instead of our time?

Physics shows that energy comes from four key areas within one's self: the body, emotions, mind, and spirit. Within each of these places, energy can be expanded and regularly renewed by establishing intentional behaviors that become subconscious. Rather than trying to manage your time with calendars, to-do lists, and time-management strategies, we would be much better off learning how to manage our energy.

Four Sources of Energy

Let's face it, change takes a great deal of energy, and sustaining change takes even more. Therefore, learning how to manage your energy is one of the biggest keys to being able to build the new habits required to achieve your desired outcomes. Several years ago, Wachovia Bank took a group of employees through a pilot energy-management program that measured performance based on the key that we drive energy. What they discovered was that those who focused on managing their energy regularly outperformed those who managed their time, in both a set of financial metrics and more intangible metrics such as customer relationship, engagement, and personal satisfaction.[8]

Body Energy

Body (or physical) energy can be increased through practices such as adequate nutrition, exercise, sleep, and rest. Rest seems to be a difficult one for many people. A practical way to engage in rest is to schedule interval breaks throughout the day. We have 90- to 120-minute cycles called ultradian rhythms, when our body cycles through low- and high-energy states. Think of it like a bank account. If we are consistently taking money out of our account and never putting anything back, we

---

8 Tony Schwartz and Catherine McCarthy, "Manage Your Energy and Not Your Time," *Harvard Business Review*, October 2007, https://hbr.org/2007/10/manage-your-energy-not-your-time.

will eventually run out of money. Our bodies are the same way. Therefore, it is important to schedule our day to support these cycles.

Practical ways of doing this would be to schedule your work in 90- to 120-minute segments, take rest breaks throughout the day (naps in the afternoon have actually been proven to increase performance), and change up your focus regularly. This same principle is why intermittent fasting helped me lose weight better than restricting calories. Our bodies need to have periods of rest when they aren't processing food (science shows that at least thirteen hours can have important health benefits).[9]

Emotional Energy

In chapter 4, we talked quite a bit about the impact of our emotions. Our emotions impact the overall quality of the energy we exert. The more we can manage our emotional energy, the more we can improve the quality of our energy despite any external pressures. We do this by being aware of our emotions and the impact they have on our overall effectiveness.

Breathing is a simple and practical way to manage your emotional energy. Heightened emotions take a great deal of energy, so by taking deep abdominal breaths and then exhaling slowly for a few seconds, it allows you to relax and turns off the fight-or-flight response that causes stress. Laughing can have this same effect, so if you experience a challenging situation that causes heightened emotion, try laughing at it. You can also use other powerful tools we've covered in past chapters, such as positive declarations, expressing appreciation or gratitude, and reflection.

---

9 Periods of fasting can protect against obesity and diabetes, ScienceDaily. com, https://www.sciencedaily.com/releases/2018/08/180831130131.htm.

Mind Energy

In chapter 4 we talked about how we cannot effectively multitask unless the action has become an automatic, subconscious habit. Therefore, trying to do too many things at one time undermines productivity. Distractions can be extremely costly, since bouncing between focuses can increase the amount of time to accomplish a task by as much as 25 percent.[10]

This is why it is important to limit your options, focus on the critical one or two things that would have the biggest impact, and organize your time around ultradian sprints, such as 90- to 120-minute segments, 2-week sprints, or 90-day focuses. This can be done by taking time each day to identify the top priority for each day and to start your day by doing that. In a meeting setting, it can be accomplished by identifying the most important one or two challenges that need to be solved in that meeting and then limiting the time to discuss the solutions to shorter timeframes.

Spiritual Energy

Spiritual energy is the energy that is derived from finding meaning and purpose that is beyond ourselves. We talked about this in chapters 2 and 3. We tap into this energy every day when the work we are doing is consistent with the things that we value most (mission, values, vision, and purpose). In chapter 2 we talked about Maslow's hierarchy of needs, which presupposes that we are created to not only live out our best selves, but to leave a legacy by helping others live out theirs.

Workforce studies consistently show that doing meaningful work and feeling valued and involved are two of the primary drivers of engagement, commitment, and satisfaction. However,

10 https://affect.media.mit.edu/pdfs/16.Mark-CHI_Email.pdf.

we tend to get caught up in the high demands and fast pace of our lives and don't leverage this incredibly powerful way of driving the energy needed for lasting change.

As Maslow's hierarchy shows, we need to be able to take care of our most basic needs first before we can start to see the value of tapping into our deeper needs. However, simple ways to get there would be to take time to reflect on our personal mission, values, and vision, and to align them to our organization's mission, vision, and values. Or think about past experiences when we were in our sweet spot, then unpack the attributes, mindsets, actions, and environment that existed and integrate them into our current circumstance or change goal (this is an example of "acting as if").

Throughout this book I have given several examples where leaders in our training programs have cited this process as the number one catalyst for their success. Aligning what is important to them personally with what is important to the organization is a powerful way to drive spiritual energy needed for change.

Driving Forces

One of the ways that we help leaders manage their energy is to understand their primary motivations. We call these their driving forces, which is one of the layers of self that I mentioned in chapter 4. While we can clearly observe different styles of behavior, it's the drivers or motivation behind those behaviors that truly explain why we do the things we do. Our driving forces can be thought of as the areas of life that we are passionate about or things we perceive as important.

A person's driving forces provide their purpose and direction in life. This is our heart layer of self. We all have various levels of energy that come from how we value and approach six things—information and truth, the use of resources (time, money, energy, and things), subjective experiences, serving others, impact and winning, and ways of doing things (methodologies and systems). Based on these unique combinations of driving forces, what creates energy for one person may take away energy for another. Because of this, our driving forces impact what we value, how we feel respected, what we trust, and what motivates us to act. A majority of the healthy and unhealthy conflict that we talked about in chapter 3 comes from this layer of self.

For example, I am driven by return-on-investment, results, and big impact. Therefore, I lose energy quickly if I don't see a return on my efforts and can't quantify the significance or impact of what I am doing, so it is important for me to objectively focus, go after little wins and improvements, and take on big challenges. I am actually energized by conflict, because it shows me we are moving forward. I serve others by treating them individually, expecting them to learn and grow, and pushing them to stretch themselves beyond where they are at today.

In contrast, my daughter is driven by subjective experience and serving others with no expectation tied to it. She will use countless hours and resources to create the best experience, help someone, or work as a team. For her, it isn't about efficiency, change, winning, or challenging. What motivates me demotivates her! If I were to expect her to do things in the same way that motivates me, she would shut down and get nothing accomplished. So when she does her chores, she does gymnastics through the kitchen (experience), makes sure that all the kids are on the same page and treated fairly (serving others and collaboration), and gets it done in her own time (not caring about efficiency, little wins, or improvements). Both ways of doing things can accomplish great results if we individually align them to what drives energy inside of us.

Practically, you can recognize your driving forces by looking at what drives the most energy, what you are passionate about, what things frustrate you, what you trust, and how you want to be respected. However, to get to the root of these driving forces more quickly, I recommend that you use an assessment. The Unstoppable website has different types of driving-forces assessments and resources that can help you identify your primary driving forces and understand how to use them to drive more energy and create more change in your life.

In the meantime, the next time you do something—anything at all—stop for a moment and ask yourself why you were driven to do what you did. Becoming aware of what drives you into action will help you better understand yourself and why you do the things you do.

APPLY: Key Questions & Activation

- How can you harness the power of intention to start "acting as if" your desired change has already been achieved? What attributes or ways of doing things can you start doing today?
- What are one to three key best practices or benchmarks that you can consider as you start to walk out your desired change?
- What is the minimally viable product, or most basic version, of your change that you can get started with today? What assumptions do you need to test as you walk out your change? How can you break your change down into smaller learning segments (90- to 120-minute segments, 2-week sprints, 90-day focuses)? How will you learn and adapt (pivot) along the way?

- What is your unique behavioral style (how you do things) that you need to consider as you walk out your change? What drives energy for you (body, emotional, mind, and spiritual)? How can you regularly increase that energy to ensure your success along the way?
- What are one to three key takeaways from this chapter that you need to share with somebody else? Teach at least one other person about these takeaways.

Go to www.wearetheunstoppable.com to find simple and practical tools that can help you make and sustain your change.

- Download worksheets that will help you identify what you need to start, stop, and continue doing; help you form new habits; develop an MVP for your change; and understand what is needed to drive the most energy for your change.
- Take an assessment that will help you identify your unique driving forces.
- Register for online courses on getting unstuck and creating new habits that will help you make and sustain your desired change.

Chapter 6

PROFICIENCIES

What Strengths, Knowledge, and Skills Do I Need to Maximize My Change?

Have you ever taken a class, or even taken part in a training program, to learn a new skill, only to find that you weren't able to get the results you expected? Or have you ever been strong at a skill in one season, only to find it isn't as strong in another? Do you tend to focus on your weaknesses rather than maximize your strengths?

All of these are common experiences, especially for people who are going through change. Often, change makes us ask, "How did I end up here?" because it highlights areas in our life that we perceive as weaknesses. Then, because we see our weaknesses as the cause for pain or loss in our lives, we conclude the best way to avoid experiencing that pain again is to work on our weaknesses.

As humans we are wired to continually improve. However, over the years we have gotten it all wrong. When we focus on improving our weaknesses, it only gets us to mediocre. But if we focus on our strengths, we have the potential to become great.

Shifting to this perspective helps us realize that most learning programs assist us in becoming who we are not, rather than helping us to be more of who we are.

My goal in this chapter is to help you make this shift. The key questions you should try to answer along the way are: What strengths can I leverage? What weaknesses can I offset? What knowledge and skills do I need to develop or outsource to be successful? Doing this will help reinforce the practices, or habits, you identified in chapter 5 that will lead you to your desired change, multiplying the effects of that change by developing your skills, competencies, and strengths.

Too often we attempt to learn a new skill without having the fundamental building blocks that will ensure mastery and sustainability. We read a new book, take a class, or try to muscle our way through things that don't come naturally in hopes of improving ourselves. We live in a world of self-help, get-rich-quick, take-a-pill-and-it-will-all-change solutions that result in mediocrity and failure.

However, becoming proficient at skills is not about rolling up your sleeves and muscling through until you master new things. This chapter will show you the common myths about building skills, and lay out several keys that will help you focus on the right skills, accelerate your mastery, and ensure sustainability.

Myth #1: Developing Skill before Mindset

One of the biggest mistakes I see leaders make when they are trying to change is to go learn a new skill without having the other P's in place first. They think that by gaining new knowledge, reading a book, or taking a class they will be able to develop the skills they need for change. However, if you learn a new skill without aligning it to your passion (mission, vision, or values), the skill has no purpose.

Mastering a skill is like building a muscle. It takes time, focus, and persistence. But why invest time, focus, and persistence to master something that you aren't passionate about or that doesn't align to your *why*? Why spend hours learning a new thing if it doesn't get you to where you want to go?

As well, you can take a class to learn something new, but if you don't have the right mindset to support that skill, you won't be able to sustain it. This is exactly what happened to me in the example I gave before when, after Rob died, I suddenly had a real challenge with solving problems and making decisions. How could it happen that the skill I had mastered over the past forty-five years had become such a great weakness almost overnight?

The answer is simple: My mindset changed about solving problems. I no longer saw them as opportunities. Rather, I saw them as overwhelming and scary. I took an assessment to pinpoint the problem and worked to correct it with declarations. Within weeks, my peers commented that I was back to being myself again.

All it took for my mastered skill to come back was the right mindset. How often do we spend countless hours trying to master a skill for which we have the wrong mindset? Without the right mindset, we'll fall short of the skill we want to achieve.

Myth #2: Good versus Great

For the past twenty years, I have been using leadership and skill assessments to help leaders discover how they are wired, their unique strengths, and their opportunities for improvement. These assessments' intent is to find the gold inside each person that can be leveraged into greatness. However, inevitably, most of the leaders I meet with focus on their weaknesses.

They focus on the things they don't like about themselves, the words that society has deemed bad, or the skills that score "lower" than others. I am always amazed at how many times I start an assessment review with someone telling me that they hated reading the assessment, that it inaccurately described them, or that it pointed out all their flaws, but after we review the results, they realized that the assessment was actually spot on. Many say the assessment has read their mail, if you know what I mean, and they are excited because they have discovered the power of their strengths in the short time we were together.

We have been trained from childhood to focus on our weaknesses, settle for what we are good at, and try to be all things to all people, rather than focus on what we could be really great at, and this leaves us tired, discouraged, and complacent.

As I said before, focusing on our weaknesses only elevates us to mediocre. We can compare it to a chain, which is only as strong as its weakest link. Often we approach our skills and habits in a way that is akin to trying to insert a weak link (or several weak links) into a chain, typically because we feel obligated to for some reason. Then we ignore the links that contribute strength, and spend all our time trying to strengthen the weak link or links that don't belong in the first place.

What if we could create good thoughts and habits without them needing to be a compensation for any weakness? In reality, we can do this, and because of how our brains work, the more we focus on our strengths, the stronger they become.[1] Also, if you think about it, as Peter Demarest and Harvey Schoof point out,

---

1 Demarest and Schoof, *Answering the Central* Question, 59.

a weakness is a strength you don't have, and it's pretty hard to do anything with something you don't have.[2]

That being said, we want to be careful about just focusing on our strengths. If we aren't aware of our weaknesses, then we won't know how to find ways to offset them. When we know our weaknesses, we will be more coachable; more able to find ways to offset them through systems, processes, tools, and help from other people; and more able to fail forward. No matter how strong we become at anything, we will still make mistakes. We will never be perfect, and understanding our weaknesses will help us learn from failures so that even our lowest moments become stepping-stones toward our goals.

Knowing our weaknesses also gives us the opportunity to involve others and gain benefit from their areas of strength. Just as our weakness could be their strength, our strength could be their weakness. We will always need others to complement and complete us. The best teams are made of individuals who can use their strengths for each other's benefit, instead of being a group of people all trying to match each other's mediocrity.

Myth #3: I Am Too Old to Learn

For centuries there has been an ongoing debate about whether nature is more important than nurture. One thing that has become clear, though, is that both are critical. We are born with certain personalities, but at the same time our brain is continually growing and adapting. Experience, training, and personal effort will always have the potential to take us further than our personality and wiring can by themselves.[3]

---

2 Ibid., 60.
3 *Mindset*, 5.

In fact, the latest research shows that the brain is a lot like a muscle, changing and getting stronger when we use it. The more we practice and learn new things, the more our brain forms new connections, which multiply and get stronger. The more we challenge our brain, the more it grows. This means that, no matter how old we are, we are still able to do things that we once thought to be hard or even impossible. Things like speaking a foreign language or learning higher math can actually become easy.[4]

So stay engaged with continuous learning. No matter what you are working to learn, simply exercising your brain will help you strengthen those mental connections that keep your brain resilient and strong, no matter your age.

Myth #4: Working Hard versus Working Smart

Work harder. Practice more. Muscle through it. You can learn or do anything. These are common themes in self-help books on change and peak performance. While they are all true in part, they don't always lead to the mastery of skill. In his book *Outliers*, Malcolm Gladwell unpacks the differentiating factors between people who have realized extraordinary success versus those who have not. One of the principles that he outlines is the 10,000-Hour Rule, which holds that it takes 10,000 hours of deliberate practice to master a skill or become world-class in any field.[5]

Ten thousand hours? That would equate to ninety minutes per day for twenty years! Who has that kind of time? I sure don't! Daunting realities like that are what keep us from making any type of change.

While the point of Gladwell's 10,000-Hour Rule is that when

---

4   *Mindset*, 219.
5   Malcolm Gladwell, *Outliers* (New York: Little, Brown and Company, 2008).

one deliberately builds a muscle over a long period of time, the likelihood of success increases greatly. In chapter 5, we talked about the importance of repetition and practice in order to create new habits. This is helpful because it reminds us to be patient with ourselves in the learning process, but the full answer doesn't lie in just needing enough time and practice to master a skill. This rule doesn't explain why some people spend countless hours practicing a skill only to never master it. It fails to ask the question about the relationship between deliberate practice and innate natural talent.

To better understand peak performance, scientists have studied expert-level performers to better understand the keys, aside from deliberate practice, that helped them master their skills. An interesting discovery was discovered. In his research, human performance psychologist K. Anders Ericsson found that some masters practiced for over twenty-five thousand hours, while others mastered skills in a fraction of the ten thousand hours that Gladwell proposed. Additionally, the research found countless others who logged more than ten thousand hours yet never seemed to attain mastery, concluding that how you practice matters far more than how much time you spend practicing.[6]

Additionally, studies in both science and psychology are repeatedly showing us new, or at least more nuanced, ways of learning based on individualized ways of learning. These personalized ways of learning can help us become proficient, expert, masterful, or at least very good in a specific skill in a lot less time than previously thought. I wonder how much of those ten thousand hours go toward helping people simply believe they can do the new skill they are trying to learn. How many hours does it

---

6   K. Anders Ericsson, 'The Role of Deliberate Practice in the Acquisition of Expert Performance

take before a person experiences their light-bulb moment and says, "Hey, maybe I really can do this!" In other words, how many hours could someone trim off from the ten thousand if they focused on creating the right mindset first?

After all, we already know it takes at least seven times of practicing or trying something in repeated intervals before we will be able to use it, and that getting our attitude under control normally takes about twenty-one days, of which the first four are the hardest.[7] While that might sound like a lot, compare it to ninety minutes a day for twenty years. The truth is, yes, the more we practice anything, the better we will get at it, but the truth also is that if we engage our minds in the process, not just the skills, then our weaknesses will diminish, our strengths will become stronger, and we will soon perform better, create greater value, and provide ourselves with evidence that we can learn and do things beyond our previous limits.

Kobe Bryant is one of the most successful basketball players of all time. I once read a story about how he would get up early to condition for up to seven hours before a game. He would condition, run, sprint, lift weights, and then make eight hundred jump shots![8] However, it wasn't his regular practice that made him great. Rather, it was his deliberate focus on building on his strengths. If you look at the practices of the top performers in every industry, you will likely find this same dynamic—a deliberate focus on practicing a critical skill backed up by reinforcing repetition.

It would be nice if we could just have a rule that said, "Work this long at anything and you'll master it," but it isn't that simple. The best approach to strengthening our skills is always

---

7 Leaf, *The Gift in You*, 159.
8 "5 Lessons We Can Learn From NBA Legend Kobe Bryant," Medium.com, https://medium.com/swlh/5-lessons-we-can-learn-from-nba-legend-kobe-bryant-7a7c73f3329d.

going to be individualized and nuanced by who we are, how we are wired, what strengths and weaknesses we already have, and more. The bottom line is that it doesn't pay off to just muscle your way through a difficulty. If you stop and consider what smarter way there may be to address your need, you will almost always improve the learning process.

ASSESS: Where Are You At?

Think about the change you want to make.

- Think about the skills and strengths you need to master. What mindsets might be preventing you from being able to master them?
- As you are thinking about your strengths and weaknesses, what do you notice first? Which do you put the most focus on? If it is your weaknesses, then you may have the wrong focus, which will lead to mediocrity.
- What are the areas in your life that you feel you "have arrived" and no longer need to learn? Perhaps these areas are the very ones you need to focus on.
- Where could you put more specific and focused effort on developing your strengths?
- Pay attention to the heightened emotions that rise up as you are reflecting on your strengths and weaknesses.

ALIGN: Keys for Success

If the four commonly held myths I mentioned hinder people from mastering skills and making or sustaining their desired change, what truths would help us? Here are some critical keys to guide you in identifying, mastering, and sustaining skills over time.

Identify and Align with the Right Skills to Master

Focus is the key to mastering any skill. As noted earlier, we can't be all things to all people. In order to be great, we need to be willing to let go of things that we might be good at. When maximizing your performance, you need to start by asking three key questions.

First, "Who am I developing this skill for, what is its purpose, and why is it important?" Start by thinking about who the customer is by asking who will receive the benefit of the skill. Is it you? Your spouse? Your boss? Your customer? By identifying the most critical stakeholders, you can determine the value mastering that skill will bring.

Second, "What skill(s) are most critical?" In chapter 5 we talked about the importance of focusing on the critical few things that will give you the greatest results. Take time to identify which skills need to be mastered in order to drive the greatest amount of progress toward reaching your desired change. It is better to start with the critical few skills, rather than trying to tackle too much and ending in failure.

Break it down into sub-skills. I often hear people say they want to grow in general skills, like communication or accountability. However, these are broad skills with many facets of sub-skills. John Hayes, a cognitive psychologist from Carnegie Mellon University, has been a thought leader in research related to the best way of mastering skills through deliberate practice. This research focuses on improving larger, more general skills by focusing mostly on improving the sub-skills that the overall skill is composed of.[9] For example, some of the sub-skills of communication are understanding others, empathy, influencing,

9 https://www.opencolleges.edu.au/informed/features/the-truth-about-deliberate-practice/.

persuasion, negotiating, and coaching. Breaking it down also makes it easier to focus on the best sub-skill that will drive the greatest results and allow you to measure results more effectively. This is an example of the deliberate practice that was mentioned previously.

Third, "Do I really need to master this skill?" The key to answering this question is to know your strengths. Science shows that when you know your strengths and begin using them, your brain becomes more efficient and your weaknesses actually become stronger because your brain no longer needs to compensate for receiving new information.[10]

Finally, if you have weaknesses that are necessary for you to be great at your goal, job, or life, don't focus on them. Rather, think about how you can leverage a resource (system, process, tool, or person) to help you be effective with the skill or find a person who has the very strength that you lack to help you.

Recently, I was working with a new supervisor who wanted to grow in his leadership ability. While determining what skills he needed to develop, he was listing things like time management, accountability, and problem solving. These were all skills that he felt he should have as a leader. They were also skills he felt he was weakest at. In fact, he had attempted to develop these skills several times in the past.

I challenged him to go back to his mission, values, and vision, as well as to consider the purpose and desired outcomes that he had related to his development plan. He suddenly realized that his purpose was to be a role model for others, and the customer of his development in this case was both his direct reports and his family.

He quickly realized that they weren't going to benefit from

him focusing on better time management, accountability, and problem solving. Instead, he focused on developing his strengths of relationship building, encouragement, and problem solving. Specifically, he focused on getting to know his reports personally, catching them doing things well, and learning how to ask questions and coach them versus telling them what to do. The amazing thing was that by building on those strengths, the other skills of time management, accountability, and problem solving also improved naturally.

Be Coachable and Accountable

In order to develop, it is important to stay coachable and open to feedback, new ideas, and new ways of doing things. Studies have shown that learning is most efficient when people are actively involved either physically or mentally in the learning process with others. Going through change with others helps us to be open to new possibilities and keeps us accountable to the change we desire. It also stretches us to go beyond where we would tend to go on our own.

This can be done in a variety of ways—through taking a class, joining a peer group, or engaging with others on social media like Facebook. As the use of technology increases, there are more tools, applications, and virtual gaming available to help reinforce your learning.

A few months into my weight-loss journey, I decided to add more intense exercise and strength building to my daily routine. However, at the gym I would become overwhelmed by the number of machines, classes, and options available to me. I didn't know the best practices required for this stage of my journey, and I was struggling with knee problems that required some accommodations to my routine.

I decided to join a paid intermediate-level cardio and

strength-training class. I had the option of several free classes, but I knew I wouldn't go if I didn't invest the extra resources. I also knew that I was wired to prefer smaller groups of familiar people, versus a larger class where everyone could show up. Plus, this class had a personal trainer who would come alongside the class and help with any necessary accommodations.

I quickly realized that this class was going to push me way beyond where I would have gone on my own. As well, the group became cheerleaders for each other. If I didn't show up for class, they would hold me accountable on our private Facebook group and would ask about my progress when I returned to class. It reinforced the importance of finding a support group to accelerate my desired change and make it more fun.

Experiential Learning: Show, Do, and Teach

One of the biggest accelerators of skill mastery is experiential learning. Studies have shown that sustainable learning and retention happens best within participatory teaching methods, such as group discussion, practice, and teaching others. In fact, these methods of learning have been proven to result in 50 to 90 percent retention rates, whereas more passive teaching methods, such as lectures, reading, audio-visual, and demonstration, only lead to 5 to 30 percent retention rates.[11]

Dr. David A. Kolb, known for his contribution to the study of education and learning, published a learning theory in 1984 that has come to be known as "See one, do one, teach one,"[12] or what I have called "Show, do, teach" over the years. The goal of this theory, widely used especially for medical trainees, is to accelerate the

---

11 https://www.educationcorner.com/the-learning-pyramid.html.
12 Kolb, D.A. (1984). *Experiential Learning: Experience as the Source of Learning and Development*. Englewood Cliffs, NJ: Prentice-Hall.

mastery of skills through three stages of experiential learning. In short, the idea is to learn a skill, engage in doing it, and then purposefully demonstrate or teach it to someone else. Each step in this process rapidly moves from the least-effective passive teaching methods to the most-effective participatory teaching methods.

It also helps us stay aligned to our individual mission, because we are all wired to ultimately find fulfillment by helping others discover their own fulfillment. By teaching others what we have learned, we are able to continuously live in a place of fulfillment.

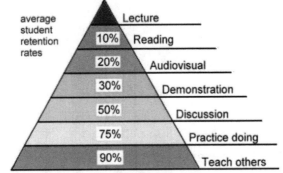

Learning Pyramid

Source: National Training Laboratories, Bethel, Maine

Show: Concrete Learning

The first stage in concrete learning is the knowledge stage, where the learner encounters a new experience or reinterprets an existing experience. This can come through learning new knowledge, looking at something through a different mindset or lens, or pulling different sub-groups of skills together to learn a new collective skill. Whenever you read something new, sit in a class, or watch somebody do something, you are in this stage of learning. Through reading, listening, or observing, you are learning something new.

However, unless you move to the next stage, you will likely only remember 5 to 30 percent of what you learned. Also, you may have knowledge, but you won't have understanding of the subject you are learning. This is because of the principles we talked about in chapters 4 and 5 related to reinforced thought and repetitive action.

Practical ways to improve your learning and retention in this stage are to develop and practice the skills of active listening, contextual thinking (applying what you are learning to a model, context, or past experience), or asking powerful questions (seeking to understand at a deeper level).

Do: Reflective Observation and Deliberate Practice

Once a person has learned new knowledge, it is time for them to gain understanding of that knowledge. There are two key parts to this stage: reflective observation and deliberate practice. This is the reflective-observation stage, where the learner applies their knowledge to real-life situations and then reflects on the results.

We have talked about the science behind both of these principles in chapters 4 and 5. However, here I will help you put them into practice with regard to learning and developing strengths.

Many people have good intentions about growing and improving. However, good intentions only turn into reality when they align to why we want to change, our perceptions (mindsets) around change, and the right activities and habits needed to sustain that change. Therefore, in order to achieve peak performance, one must move quickly from intent, learning, or new knowledge (being shown) to practicing (doing).

Reflective Observation. Reflective observation is the ability to test your new knowledge or skill in various environments to see how it responds and then to adapt the application of that knowledge or skill to fit the need. It is like building a muscle. In

UNSTOPPABLE

order to strengthen your learning, you need to challenge it, think about it, and try it out in various situations. Too often, people fail to intentionally understand what they are learning, why they are learning it, and whom they are learning it for. The result is that they do for the sake of doing instead of being able to harness the power of this stage to observe and reflect on the progress and results of the new skill.

I have made a practice of this throughout all areas of my life. For example, when I am listening to a sermon at church each week, I listen for the key points being made. Then I set aside time to think about how those points would fit in my daily life and in business. The "churchy" words may not be the same as the words I use in business, but I have found that the principles I am learning there are the same principles that drive high performance in business. By taking the time to apply this new learning to a context I know, it reinforces my ability to understand and live those principles more effectively. Plus, it makes the new things that I am learning more relevant because I have context and experience to support the learning.

Deliberate Practice. Earlier we talked about the importance of deliberate practice in order to master new learning and skills. When you practice a sequence of ideas or movements over and over, you help your brain form and strengthen patterns of connections.[13] Neuroscientists have identified deliberate practice as a primary way to become an elite performer. It so happens that the basic properties that define deliberate practice are valuing the change, being observant and self-aware, focusing on specific sub-skills, repetition, reflection and feedback, and celebrating progress.[14] These are all the principles we have talked about in

13 Mind sculpture, 102.
14 Demarest and Schoof, *Answering the Central Question*, 70.

chapters 2 through 5. It isn't just about the number of hours you practice. Rather, it is about applying that practice to something familiar and meaningful.

As I come alongside leaders to help them turn around and grow their companies, I often find they have some sort of management system in place that provides them with tools and resources to meet goals, make decisions, and organize their work. While this system is great (we offer similar types of systems, tools, and resources to our clients), typically there isn't the necessary understanding of these systems to reinforce and sustain the learning.

What could be a very powerful, collective tool for managing instead becomes a crutch. In fact, I have sat in some meetings that felt somewhat like a cult. If someone didn't follow the system precisely or check the box, they would be chastised for not following the rules. In those meetings, there was little or no understanding of the purpose and intent of those tools, and these teams would spend way too much time going through the motions and never actually get to solving any real problems.

Teach: Active Experimentation and Teaching

These leaders were doing the work. They even had some level of understanding. As a result, they may have been getting it 30 to 50 percent right. However, they lacked the wisdom that comes in the teaching stage of learning.

Teaching is the stage of sustainable learning where the person applies their learning in a way that models what they have learned and teaches others to do the same. This is where wisdom is developed and learning retention can reach its peak. This can be done through simply telling someone about what we learned or the impact it had on us, or engaging them in learning the knowledge or skills themselves.

It is believed that Albert Einstein once said, "If you can't explain it to a six-year-old, you don't understand it yourself." We can know facts and develop basic skills but not have the ability to apply those skills effectively in the right situations. Additionally, we may understand how to apply those skills effectively in situations but not have true wisdom in how to apply them masterfully. This wisdom comes through active experimentation by talking about what we have learned, modeling it, and teaching it to others.

A big part of turning around and accelerating the growth of companies is teaching next-generation leaders how to lead. It is one thing to be an effective, intuitive leader. It is another to know how to teach leadership. That's why all our training tools, resources, and programs integrate this type of experiential learning into them.

Over the years, we have developed and delivered dozens of several high-performance leadership and coaching certification programs, apprenticeship programs, courses, and coaching programs. In all of these, the single most important element that reinforces learning is when the students tell somebody about what they learned, model it for them, or walk beside them as they learn it themselves. This is why we have recommended that you tell somebody about what you have learned in the *apply* section of each chapter of this book. The more you share what you are learning, the more you will reinforce it within yourself.

Know Your Learning Style

In order to maximize your learning and skill development, it is important to understand your unique learning style. In learning theory, there are several different models of learning styles. However, for the sake of this book it is important to reflect and recognize the ways that you best learn in order to accelerate and maximize your results.

The first thing to think about is what senses drive the greatest level of learning within you. Some people are visual learners; they learn and understand best when they see what they are learning—a model or a visual. Others are auditory learners; they learn best when they hear information and can internalize concepts. Some are kinesthetic learners; they learn and understand best when they experience learning through hands-on experience.

Most children are kinesthetic learners, which is why interactive play is so important to their development. However, humans develop additional learning styles as they mature. As people develop and mature, more unique learning styles emerge. By the time a child is thirteen or fourteen years old, their primary learning style is usually developed.

We talked about your unique behavioral style in chapter 5. Since both behavioral and learning styles are based on the same layer of self, I encourage you to refer to chapter 5 as you consider the individual learning style that will optimize your performance.

There are four primary learning styles that will emerge. Some people learn best in fast-paced environments that involve big-picture ideas and independent learning environments. Others may prefer fast-paced, interactive, and fun learning environments that involve learning with others and group projects. Some may prefer flexible, slower-paced, one-on-one learning environments that provide support people and resources. Others may prefer slow-paced, structured learning environments that allow for learning, testing, and understanding lots of details. Depending on your style, you will want to structure your learning environment to accelerate and reinforce the learning style that is best for you.

APPLY: Key Questions & Activation

Reflect on your desired change. With your mission, vision, values, and desired outcomes in mind, consider the following:

- What one to three skills do you need to develop or master to make your desired change, achieve your desired outcomes, and fulfill your vision? What are the most critical sub-skills that will accelerate your ability to develop your desired skills?
- What weaknesses would be better to offset through others, systems, or processes?
- How can you be more accountable and coachable to developing these skills?
- How can you best learn (show) these necessary skills? Immediately practice (do) them? And tell or show (teach) someone else how to do them?
- What are one to three key takeaways from this chapter that you need to share with somebody else? Teach at least one other person about these takeaways.

Go to www.wearetheunstoppable.com to find simple and practical tools that can help you make and sustain your change.

- Download worksheets that will help you identify the strengths you need to reinforce and the weaknesses you need to offset.
- Download RX Worksheets for specific skills you want to master.

- Register for online courses on getting unstuck and creating new habits that will help you make and sustain your desired change.
- Check out the High-Performance Leadership, Coaching Manager Certification, and apprenticeship programs that are available to help you develop yourself or your leaders.

Chapter 7

PLATFORM

What Culture, Support, and Accountability Do I Need to Ensure Sustainable Change?

Have you ever made a big change, only to go back into your environment and find that it is difficult to sustain, hard for others to support, or difficult to integrate into the rest of your life? I have found this to be true in my own life.

Platform is something people often don't think about when they want to sustain change. They learn new skills or change habits, but they don't change their support system (systems and processes; the people who reinforce accountability for the change; and the culture, tools, and resources to support the change). Unfortunately, this makes change so much more difficult. To help address this, the key questions I want you to ask as you read this chapter are: What culture is needed for this change to be successful? What support, encouragement, and accountability is needed? Who can help hold me accountable?

When I lost my first one hundred pounds, it was during a season where I was focused on getting healthy and building relationships with my kids. My business had taken a back seat, so the focus on health was much easier. However, as I started to get more involved in business again, it was much harder to make sure I was eating healthy and getting to the gym. I needed to be intentional about building a support platform that would allow me to sustain that change and continue to lose weight, despite how my circumstances had changed. I also needed to ensure that my environment was supportive of the new change.

We also need support from others. Humans are designed to support each other. Research shows that "high levels of social support predict longevity at least as reliably as healthy eating and regular exercise do, while low levels of social support are as damaging as high blood pressure."[1] At the same time, when we support others, our own healing is increased by 63 percent.[2]

Have you ever heard the saying, "You are who you hang around with"? This speaks to the importance of intentionally building the right support network to help you make and sustain your change. Studies have shown that people who change and go back into their previous environment are less likely to sustain that change than those who don't. In fact, it has been proven that addicts who change their lives need to go into a completely different environment in order to sustain their recovery.[3]

A client that I worked with a few years ago spent a great deal of time and effort training their emerging leaders how to lead more effectively. They were empowered to make continuous

1 Leaf, *Think, Learn, Succeed*, 91.
2 Ibid., 92.
3 Ren, "Why a Complete, Life Change Is Necessary for Effective Addiction Recovery," *Narconon International*, September 2, 2018, www.narconon.org/blog/why-a-complete-life-change-is-necessary-for-effective-addiction-recovery.html.

improvement, collaborate, and empower others, and then encouraged to go back to their respective departments and be leaders. However, the supervisors within the company refused to buy into this way of leading.

As a result, their performance-management systems were either halfheartedly implemented or, in many cases, ignored. This led to even greater frustration throughout the organization. Those emerging leaders now visualized a new reality of what life could be like in the organization, yet the support, systems, structure, and rewards did not line up with the new way of doing things. In order for that change to take root and be sustained, the resistors to change needed to be removed from their leadership roles and new systems had to be communicated and reinforced.

Whether in the business world or in our personal lives, when we make a change, we also need a sustaining change in our support system.

ASSESS: Where Are You At?

Think about the change you want to make.

- What support structures (environments, people, systems, tools, or resources) do you currently have in place that will help you sustain the change you desire? Which may hurt or stifle your progress and sustainability?
- What support structures have you relied on with other changes, that may be helpful to reinforce during this one?
- Pay attention to the heightened emotions that rise as you are reflecting on these questions.

ALIGN: Keys for Success

Mentors, Coaches, and Those Who Have Gone Before

The first thing to think about when you are building your support system is, *Who are the mentors, coaches, and people who have gone before me?* We can learn a lot from those who have preceded us. Change is hard enough, so why not avoid having to recreate the wheel?

Recently, I was cycling through the Smokie Mountains. My bicycle had electric pedal assist, so that when I got fatigued, I had a little help with pedaling. I never actually used this feature, but just knowing it was there caused me to go much farther and higher than I ever would have gone without it! That is the way mentors, coaches, and those who have gone before us work. They are there to encourage us to go places we wouldn't go otherwise, to be there to give us an extra push when we feel stretched, and to be there to carry us when we get tired.

Whenever I start with any change, I make a point to seek out someone who has gone before me who would be willing to either mentor or coach me through my change. In business, that would be my CEO roundtable group, my business coach, and leaders in my industry. In my weight-loss journey, it was people who had lost more than one hundred pounds, and my wellness coach and personal trainer. Learning from others who have been in similar situations can be extremely valuable.

In a world of unlimited possibilities, we can easily feel like our situation is so unique that nobody could possibly understand what we are going through. However, the reality is that humans are wired similarly. We saw this in previous chapters, looking at the different ways of thinking, behavioral styles, and driving forces. The same is true with our life situations. We can look for themes and patterns in people's lives that will allow us to learn from and be supported by others throughout our journey.

Additionally, we have talked about the power of testimony in previous chapters. This same principle holds true with our support network. We can draw on the testimonies of others, make their ceiling our floor, and even realize a greater level of sustainable change than they did.

As a consultant, I see the power of mentorship and coaching play out all the time. One example of this was a young man who wanted to be a business owner. Instead of rushing out to start a business and "figure it out the hard way," he asked to shadow me for a season. By doing this, he was able to learn what type of business he wanted to own and the best practices for being a business owner. When he finally did step into his business, he was ready and equipped to be successful.

Support, Encouragement, and Accountability Partners

While it can be extremely beneficial to have a mentor or coach in life, other fundamental roles can also help us sustain the change we want to make. In his book *Vital Friends*, Tom Rath talks about the importance of identifying different types of people who are necessary in our life to add meaningful value.[4]

Based on the behavioral styles that we discussed in chapter 5, there are eight different types of people who can support you through various stages of your journey.[5] Think about the different relationships in your life. Who in your life helps to fulfill the following roles?

4   Tom Rath, *Vital Friends: The People You Can't Afford to Live Without* (New York: Gallup Press, 2006).
5   Target Training International, http://targettraininginternational.com/.

- **Conductors**—The people who motivate and push you to think bigger, help you get unstuck, and will guide and challenge you.
- **Persuaders**—The people who will encourage you, give you advice, connect you with others, and keep you moving forward.
- **Promoters**—The people who will accept you for who you are, pick you up when you are down, and energize you.
- **Relators**—The people who will relate to you. The first ones you call when you need a friend.
- **Supporters**—The people who are simply there to serve you, no questions asked. They will support you, encourage you, and help you.
- **Coordinators**—The people who have similar interests and motivations as you. They will roll up their sleeves and help you get things done with you, and help you ask the critical questions.
- **Analyzers**—The people who will help you see what is out of order, what could go wrong, or challenge you to think differently. They will help you ask the critical questions.
- **Implementors**—The people who will help you think differently, challenge you to think differently, and roll up their sleeves and help you get things done.

Too often, we rely on one or two people to fulfill all of these roles in our lives, then we get frustrated when they are not able to effectively support, encourage, and hold us accountable for the change we desire. We tend to expect these people to play critical roles throughout multiple seasons of life, rather than intentionally identifying and seeking out people who are the best fit for the change we want to see.

For example, when Rob passed, I found myself in a completely new season of life. As I mentioned before, I no longer had that persuader I could bounce big decisions off, who would give me advice or encourage me to keep moving forward. Previously, he and I had an agreement that regardless of what our perspectives were, if we didn't both have peace about a decision, the answer was *no* or *not now*. So, when he passed, I was paralyzed from making big decisions because not only was my mindset negatively changed, but I also hadn't identified a new persuader as a part of my support platform. For me, my faith is a guiding force, so part of regaining my ability to make decisions was determining I would go to God as my persuader. I also leaned more heavily on the trusted advisors in my life who were serving as conductors and promoters.

Then when I stepped into the goal of losing one hundred and fifty pounds, I sought out groups of people who had lost at least one hundred pounds so I would have others to be energized by, to collaborate with, and to open my mind to new possibilities. And now that I am in a different season of my journey, those roles are readjusting in my life yet again.

Another challenge to change is that we tend to only see part of a picture or situation. As a result, blind spots, limiting beliefs, and strongholds can emerge that will prevent us from making and sustaining the change we desire. Since these skewed perspectives tend to be subconscious, we need to have others in our lives who can help us recognize them for what they are. In order to successfully change—and sustain that change—we must have the right people in our lives to help us see from multiple perspectives.

For example, I know that one of the subconscious strongholds I am working on reversing is the belief that people will let me down. This shows up in my life through guardedness, lack of trust, and hesitancy to delegate or let go of control. It was accentuated when Rob died, because my mind said, "See, Michelle, everyone does let you down. Rob let you down. God let you down. And now that everyone is going back to their lives and forgetting about you, they are letting you down."

Consciously, I know those are all lies. However, subconsciously, those lies colored how I opened myself up to, interacted with, and trusted people. So I needed to be intentional about finding builders, navigators, and champions in my life who could recognize those strongholds when they popped up and give me a swift kick in the pants and a new perspective. Otherwise, my decisions about people would have all been made based on a lie and I would have never been able to make it through a difficult season of my life that hinged on my being able to trust and accept the help of others.

As you are stepping into your change journey, be sure to intentionally identify the support roles that you need to be able to navigate and sustain your desired change.

Supporting Culture

While it is important to have the right people to be able to walk beside us as we change, it is equally important to make sure the culture that reinforces our new ways also lines up with the change we desire.

For the last fifteen years, I have studied high-performing organizations. At the root of high performance (better, faster, and more efficient ways of doing things over a sustained period of time) is both positive psychology (the study of living a fulfilling life) and organizational psychology (the study of organizational structures that support high performance). Each of these point to the need for building into our environment positive structures, systems, processes, tools, and people who support the change we desire for the long term.

When combined, both of these concentrate on building cultures that emphasize strength over weakness, building on the good versus the bad, and bringing out the great instead of the good in a way that drives high performance and results. By intentionally focusing on building a positive platform, you will ensure that the change you are making can be achieved and sustained over the long haul.

In chapter 5, we talked about antecedents (the things that come before a change that set us up for success) and how important they are for driving positive results. They could be a benchmark,[6] something that has worked in the past, a driving force that will inspire us to make the change, or the information we need to make decisions. So, if positive antecedents are important for making the change, then building those positive antecedents into our support platform is critical for sustaining the change. The way we do this is by setting up structures, systems, and processes that make it easier to repeat the necessary behaviors and activities that lead toward sustainable change.

I often work with organizations that seek to achieve a new result, target a new customer segment, or develop a new strategy but fail to change the supporting structures, systems, and processes necessary to drive different results. I will hear "We already have our standard operating procedures defined," or "This is the way we have always done things." But, in reality, if we want a different result, we need to go about it a different way. Structures, systems, and processes always need to change to support the desired outcome, customer, or strategy.

The same is true in our personal lives. We tend to go through

---

6 Daniels and Daniels, *Performance Management*, 99.

the motions of change and fail to intentionally establish and align new structures, systems, and processes to reinforce and support that new change.

For example, I used to work long, focused hours. Rob worked too, but his schedule was more flexible than mine. So the kids would go to him if they needed something. When he passed, I needed to build a new relationship with the kids. The structure of my life had to change so I could be there to get my youngest on the bus, take them to their activities, and help them with their homework. I needed to build systems and processes into my daily schedule that allowed me to be available for their last-minute calls, forgotten backpacks, and sick days. I also purposed to build in regular processes that reinforced relationship, such as scheduled dinners, individual date nights with each child, and going to the gym with my son instead of going to my personal trainer. The old way of doing things would not reinforce and sustain the change I was seeking to make.

If you want to change, you need to be open to agile structures, systems, and processes. In chapter 5, we discussed the lean approach to change. This is also true with building your support platform. You need to focus in on the essential few things that will help you drive and support your change and then be open and flexible enough to change them along the way.

Reward Systems

Let's face it, change takes a lot of energy. In fact, the reason most of us get stuck, don't change, or fail to sustain change is because we lose the positive momentum and energy that keep us going through the trials, setbacks, and failures that come with long-term change. This is so important that we talked about managing our energy in chapter 5.

As mentioned previously, brain science shows us that people are wired for positivity. We have an area in our brain called the corpus striatum that is activated by positive reinforcement. When activated, it causes us to feel good, safe, and self-confident.[7] Engagement studies back up this science by showing that people are most engaged when they feel valued, involved, productive, and a part of something bigger than themselves. In fact, when people feel intrinsically valued (valued for who they are), they are 40 percent more cooperative and productive than when they feel only extrinsically valued (valued for what they do).[8]

Therefore, in order to make, reinforce, and sustain change, it is critical that we develop reward systems that feed that need for intrinsic motivation. However, we are all intrinsically motivated in different ways. This ties back to the driving forces that we discussed in chapter 5.

Psychologist David Premack, known for his theory, the Premack Principle, discovered that high-probability behaviors can be a reinforcer for low-probability behaviors. So, if we look at what people do when given a choice, we can discover key reinforcers that will incentivize behavior that is less desirable. These reinforcers can be social (quality time or affirmations), work related (job promotion, rotation, or development), or tangible (gifts, compensation, or time).[9]

This means that if we find what rewards us, we can use it to positively reinforce what we otherwise don't like or wouldn't choose to do. For example, I am a complex thinker, so writing has always felt difficult for me. When I started working on this

7   Leaf, *The Gift in You*, 147.
8   Robert S. Hartman, *The Structure of Value: Foundations of Scientific Axiology* (Carbondale: Southern Illinois University Press, 1967).
9   Daniels and Daniels, *Performance Management*, 199.

book, I would get overwhelmed and stuck quickly. However, I am driven by impact (driving force) and I love being able to see a return on my investment of time, resources, energy, and money.

The way I intentionally got through the feelings of overwhelm and being stuck with writing was to challenge myself to ninety-minute writing intervals. Once I was finished writing, I would allow myself to think about the impact that these principles will make when applied in the lives of others, and this would create enough energy to drive me beyond what felt challenging or difficult. Likewise, as I was losing weight, I would set mini goals for myself. If I met those goals, I would reward myself with fun things like new clothes, exercise equipment, or other incentives that would keep me going through the painful process of change.

Reward systems can also be a powerful tool for reinforcing change within business. Compensation is an example of a reward system meant to drive a certain type of behavior. Yet, most managers don't align this reward system to the new behaviors they are trying to reinforce and then wonder why they don't get a different result.

Compensation is an example of an extrinsic motivator. It is not the primary driver of the behavior, and, in fact, compensation typically only reinforces behavior if it serves to meet the needs of the person (Maslow's hierarchy of needs) or if it is a core motivator for the person (driving forces).

For example, one of my clients determined that they wanted their salespeople to start cross-selling. This required that the salesforce learn how to be more consultative in their approach, sell more comprehensive solutions, and sell value versus just selling off a standard price list. But the business made the change in expectations without changing the reward structure (compensation) that would reinforce those new behaviors. As a result, the company didn't get the results they needed and the salespeople ended up frustrated because they were no longer being intrinsically motivated.

However, once we slightly modified their compensation structure to reward solutions-based and value-added selling and lined it up with the individual salesperson's driving forces, their sales immediately increased and engagement went up.

Reward systems that are aligned to a person's driving forces can be a simple and practical way of driving and sustaining desired change.

Tools and Resources

Once we have found success in our change journey, it is important to develop tools and resources that will allow us to repeat our success over the long haul. Developing a toolbox of tools and resources is a simple and practical key for being able to carry out and sustain change over time. By finding tools and resources that reinforce our desired outcomes, we can simplify, organize, systematize, and repeat our change over time.

In the age of technology, support tools and resources are often easy and affordable. The key to these tools and resources is to make them as simple and user-friendly as possible. Also, in chapter 3 we talked about different levels of maturity. It is important to make sure that our tools and resources are aligned to our level of maturity. A tool that is too simple may prevent us from having the information or resources necessary to make complex change.

For example, when setting out to lose one hundred and fifty pounds, I started by using a meal plan and a macronutrient-tracking application. This worked well in the beginning. However, after I lost the first thirty pounds, weight loss became more difficult. At that point I needed to bring in more advanced tools such as DNA testing and other biometric testing that allowed me to understand my body make-up, limiting factors, and toxins that would prevent or accelerate my weight loss. If I would have started with all of these, the process probably would have overwhelmed me. However, once I was used to the initial tools, these advanced tools became more manageable and necessary to help me get to my next level of weight loss.

Throughout the last fifteen years, my company has developed and tested change-management tools and resources that have proven successful at all levels of maturity. These tools are designed to help you get unstuck, and accelerate and sustain your change in all areas of life. Go to www.wearetheunstoppable.com to find simple and practical tools that can help you make and sustain your change.

APPLY: Key Questions & Activation

Think about the change you desire:

- Who are one to three mentors, coaches, or others who have gone before you that can help support you through this change? What role should they play (refer to the different relationships types)?
- What environment or culture around you will prevent your change from lasting? What is the ideal environment or culture that will reinforce your change?
- What reinforcers of change should you build into your support structure? How are you best rewarded?
- What tools and resources could help you reinforce and sustain your change?

- What are one to three key takeaways from this chapter that you need to share with somebody else? Teach at least one other person about these takeaways.

Go to www.wearetheunstoppable.com to find simple and practical tools that can help you make and sustain your change.

- Download worksheets that will help you identify the best support people and structures to reinforce and sustain your desired change.

Chapter 8

PERFORMANCE

How Will I Know I Am Successful?

C ongratulations! By this point, you have made it through some hugely significant steps. Hopefully you are already seeing significant impact in your life from what you've learned up to this point and the work you've done to apply it.

Celebrating progress is so important, but there's only one way to know if we are making progress, and that's to measure results. Believe it or not, the idea of measuring results really excites some people. They love measuring things!

In case you are not one of those people, think back to when you were growing up. Did you have a board where you would mark your growth? Kids often get so excited to mark off their new height and see how much they've grown, especially when they're younger. Even if you didn't keep a board for measuring, do you remember how other milestones made you feel, like when your shoes were the same size as your parents' or when you started getting taller than some adults?

Measuring results should give us that same sense of excitement we had with those growth milestones as a child. Honestly, why wouldn't you be excited about seeing how successful you've been and how much you've grown? The only reason to have a negative perception about measuring results is that you expect your results to be negative, and if that's what you expect, then I would encourage you to use the tools from chapter 4 to dig deeper into that mindset and replace it with one that's confident that measuring results will lead to celebration.

To help us understand how to accurately measure results, the key questions to answer in this chapter are: How will I know if I have met my goals? Are my goals simple? Are they both leading and lagging? Whom should I communicate them to? Do these measures align to my mission, values, vision, and desired outcomes?

Measure So You Know

Once you have determined the behavior and result you desire to change, it's time to measure results. Measuring results will not only tell you how you are doing along the way, but will also create a line of sight to your bigger vision or goal. The purpose of measurement is to see the smaller changes in performance, which will allow you to reinforce your change more often. If you don't measure, you won't be able to tell if performance is getting better, worse, or staying the same; this will not only guarantee faster change but also identify poor performance. This data can give you important clues as to what needs to change in order to drive more results, faster.

Optimal performance requires reinforcement. Without effective measurement, you may think there is improvement when there really is no change, or change you don't want. You may spend unnecessary time and resources reinforcing the wrong behavior, at the wrong time, for the wrong reason. Effective measures also help you determine which reinforcers have the most positive effect on the change you want. When armed with objective data, you will be able to come up with effective solutions to your challenges, and it will remove the emotion involved with change and performance.

For example, through setting measures throughout my weight loss, I was able to determine that fasting longer between meals had more impact on the amount of weight I lost than the amount of food I ate. I also learned that too much protein impacted my weight loss just as much as too much carbohydrates. Finally, I learned that genetically I tend to favor certain foods over others. This information allowed me to adapt my diet to the right formula necessary for my body to accelerate weight loss. The icing on the cake (no pun intended) was that my energy increased and I was never hungry, so my weight-loss journey became a routine very quickly.

I wouldn't have ever known all this if I had simply measured my results by counting calories or not eating the foods I love to eat because they didn't appear to be "diet" foods. I started by measuring one or two things. Then, as I learned more about how my body responded to those variables, I would move to one or two other factors. I used apps on my phone that simplified the process, allowed me to run reports and track trends, and appealed to my competitive nature by comparing my journey to others'. Without effective measures, I would have struggled with the same old patterns that had kept me obese most of my life.

Failing Forward

Often, people associate measures with punishment. This is because bad behavior is annoying, so we attempt to change that behavior by pinpointing it and punishing it through metrics; for example, "You showed up late to work three times this week, so we're going to write you up." However, this focus on punishment has resulted in a society that is afraid of failure. This is truly unfortunate, because no change can happen unless something fails. Growth doesn't happen without something needing to die. So when we create fear of failure, we stifle creativity, innovation, growth, and change.

In reality, the greatest inventions have come from the biggest failures. The average number of failures for entrepreneurs is 3.8 before they finally make it in business.[1] Steve Jobs was fired from every company he started, yet that didn't stop him from being a visionary and a pioneer in the areas of computers and breakthrough communication. Bill Gates was a Harvard dropout, yet that hasn't stopped him from innovative strategy, entrepreneurship, and philanthropy. Albert Einstein couldn't talk until he was nine and was expelled from school, yet that didn't stop him from winning the Nobel Prize and becoming one of the greatest minds of our history. Abraham Lincoln failed in business, suffered a nervous breakdown, and experienced a lifetime of failures, yet that didn't stop him from becoming one of the greatest presidents in our country's history. I could go on and on with examples of failures turned into success. The reality is that most successful people have failed numerous times in their lives.

In his book *Failing Forward: Turning Mistakes into Stepping Stones for Success*, John C. Maxwell outlines the seven abilities needed in order to fail forward and become an achiever. Achievers simply reject rejection, don't give up or base their worth on their performance, take responsibility for their actions and don't

---

1 John C. Maxwell, *Failing Forward: Turning Mistakes into Stepping Stones for Life* (Nashville, TN: Thomas Nelson, 2000).

take failure personally, see failure as temporary, regard failure as an isolated incident, set realistic expectations, focus on their strengths and the positive aspects of a situation, and try new ways of doing things.[2] Fear of failure stops forward progress and will keep you stuck.

In her book *The Gifts of Imperfection*, Dr. Brené Brown talks about how the essence of man is imperfection. If you can embrace the fact that you're going to make mistakes, you will open yourself to creativity, innovation, and success.[3]

Poor metrics are one of the top ten reasons that people fail.[4] Effective and meaningful metrics can remove the fear that comes with failure. They allow us to identify poor performance, see ourselves clearly, look at both the good and bad reinforcers of behavior, and know when it is time to pivot and adapt our strategy or ways of doing things.

What are you afraid of that is causing you to stay stuck? To procrastinate? Or to avoid change altogether? What are you avoiding for fear of failure? And how can you embrace these areas to accelerate your change instead?

The Chinese Bamboo

Throughout this book, we have talked a great deal about our subjective reality versus actual reality. The same can be true with measuring success. Often, we *think* we are not getting results, when in reality the opposite is true.

The story of the Chinese bamboo is one of my favorite ways to give a glimpse of how our perceptions of success can be skewed

---

2 Ibid.
3 Brené Brown, *The Gifts of Imperfection: Let Go of Who You Think You Should Be and Embrace Who You Are* (Center City, MN: Hazelden, 2010).
4 Maxwell, *Failing Forward: Turning Mistakes into Stepping Stones for Success.*

without the right metrics to guide us along the way. Imagine that you have a dream to grow a beautiful Chinese bamboo tree. You have envisioned being the best bamboo farmer in the land and have strategized with your friends to come up with a plan to win awards for your magnificent creation. To do this, you diligently prepare the ground and then plant a small bamboo seed. For an entire year, you water it and fertilize it in anticipation. However, except for a tiny sprout…

Nothing happens. But you aren't a quitter. You continue to water it regularly and fertilize it with love and compassion for a second year, excited to see what your labor will bring. However, to your amazement…

Nothing happens. Frustrated, you peer at it from all sides to discern if perhaps, in some hidden place, something is growing.

Still, nothing happens. Year three rolls around and you are getting angry. You have watered it, fertilized it, and lovingly cleared the thorns and weeds away, and then…

Nothing happens. You are so discouraged. You planted your seed with love and hope. You obtained the best soil. You watered it faithfully and gave it the best fertilizer. You gave up hours of your time to invest in the hopes and dreams that your tree would grow. Now you start to wonder what your reward is for all this time and effort.

Still, nothing happens. You enter year four. You are tired and weary, starting to doubt that anything will come of your beloved tree. You imagine that it must have died in the ground, and even consider digging it up and giving up. But you decide to give it one last bit of water. You fertilize it. You care for the precious seed you planted and…

Nothing happens. You look around, noticing the other plants in the garden have grown by leaps and bounds, stunning the eyes with their vibrant growth and life, gladdening your heart and the hearts of others. Many have grown to four and five feet tall by now. Their growers get accolades for their green thumbs, while people scoff at you for wasting your time on no results. Still, with your precious bamboo seed...

Nothing happens. For four years you have seen nothing but a tiny shoot sprouting from a bulb, no bigger than it was the first year. You can empower it, encourage it, and challenge it, or get angry and throw your hands up in frustration. By now, quite honestly, you might want to stomp the life out of it. You want your four years back. Then, just when you are ready to call it quits and lay down your watering can...

Something starts to happen during the fifth year: *growth!* But you still doubt that this bamboo will amount to anything. It must be just another small shoot that will give you little hope with no reward.

Over the next six weeks, however, your tiny Chinese bamboo grows as much as three feet *per day!* Within two days, it shoots past all the other trees that once overshadowed your little dream. It grows, and grows, and grows. Others can't believe what is happening. Where did that beauty come from? Who is its green thumb? It can't be true!

Suddenly, as you visit your magnificent wonder, you realize that it has grown to be *ninety feet tall!* You walk away pondering where your faith was lost. You marvel in wonder at the beauty of your beloved tree.

Often our desired change is like the Chinese bamboo. It can be discouraging. You think you have a clear mission, values, and vision—then *nothing happens.* You take the time to clearly define your purpose and change, identify goals and desired outcomes, and set guardrails—then *nothing happens.* You work hard to reverse limiting beliefs, do all the right things, and build the right skills—then *nothing happens.* You intentionally build the right platform of support resources, tools, and people—still, *nothing happens.*

Yet during the long years when there are no visible results, you have been developing a mature, long-reaching root system that would sustain and nurture its explosive growth—growth beyond anything you could have envisioned on your own, growth beyond your wildest dreams!

This extensive network of roots takes four years to develop before the tender bamboo shoot ever breaks ground and heads for the sun. For those who continue to do things right and are not discouraged, for those who are persistent, rewards will follow. For those who have faith to step into the unknown, great things can happen. Building the right foundation is the first step to creating an organization that is able to endure for many generations. During this time, you are building the right character to sustain immense growth, break through the ceiling of your potential, and go from ordinary (maybe even good) to extraordinary.

Big change requires big roots! So, if you find that you aren't seeing the results you thought you would see, you feel like you are battling the same circumstance, or you simply feel stuck, I encourage you to dig deeper to look for the root system that may be forming under the surface.

ASSESS: Where Are You At?

Think about the change you want to make.
- What would tell you that you are successful with your desired change?
- What fears surface as you think about measuring your results?
- What are some of the underlying changes that need to happen before you can see tangible results? How can you measure those?

- Pay attention to the heightened emotions that rise as you are reflecting on these questions.

ALIGN: Keys for Success

Establishing metrics can feel overwhelming and complicated. Yet, with the right metrics you can get unstuck, know when to pivot and adapt, and accelerate the success of your desired change. Over the years, I have identified a few keys that can improve the success of establishing and making effective decisions from metrics.

Make Metrics Matter

Metrics are intended to reinforce positive behaviors that lead to your desired change. Therefore, the changes you measure need to line up to your foundational mission, values, and vision. Not only will this ensure that you move toward your goal, but it will also eliminate the fear of being punished for not meeting your goal. When you have metrics that matter, you get results that matter.

Over the last two years, one of my goals has been to increase the stewardship of my financial resources. Rob and I always had a goal to get to a place where we would give away over half of our income to meaningful causes. We started by simplifying life and tithing (giving 10 percent of what we earned) despite our circumstances. This was important to us because we were both passionate about bringing out the gold in others and helping them impact the world through entrepreneurship.

However, when Rob passed, a great deal of fear related to money crept up on me. I realized I had limiting beliefs that were telling me I needed to protect what I had because I was now the only provider. To reverse that limiting belief, I set a metric around my giving. I tracked the number of times I intentionally gave beyond what felt comfortable, as well as the emotions that rose up in those situations, so I could get to the root of the lie that I needed to reverse in order to be able to give more.

I could have simply tracked how much I gave or the increase of my giving over time, but that metric wouldn't have been meaningful to me. Rather, by setting a metric that uncovered and unrooted the lies preventing me from giving more and a metric that tracked the times I gave through a place of discomfort, it tapped into my purpose of making a big impact in the lives of people. By having metrics that mattered, I started to reverse the thinking that kept me stuck and I have increased the amount of giving that matters.

Driving Forces

In chapter 5 we talked about the importance of driving forces to reinforce the new behaviors necessary for change. These driving forces can also be applied to metrics. Metrics are meant to tell us whether or not we are successful in moving toward our desired change. However, because metrics can elicit fear of failure or punishment, it is important to ensure that your metrics continue to drive energy, passion, and momentum. Aligning your metrics to your driving forces will help you do this.

For example, if you are driven by utility (return-on-investment), then you will be driven by metrics that show how quickly, efficiently, or practically you are doing something. I am driven by utility. So, as I was writing this book, one of my metrics was the number of words I was able to write in a given amount of time. I am also driven by power, so I don't like to settle for insignificant results. Therefore, I knew I was successful if I was able to find the right formula for getting the most amount of words with the biggest impact.

This became both a leading and lagging indicator of the

progress I was making (these terms are explained later in this chapter), which helped me plan my next writing days. However, this metric could actually be very demotivating to someone who is driven by low utility or low power. A better metric for those driving forces would be the amount of collaborative efforts that went into writing the book or getting the writing done quickly so I could spend time with people.

The table below shows some examples of different types of metrics that would drive passion, energy, and momentum for the twelve different driving forces.

	High	**Low**
Knowledge	Intellectual Objective, facts & data, research, best practices, true/false	Instinctive Subjective, experience, litmus test
Utility	Resourceful Numbers, increase, efficiency, return-on-investment, simple, practical	Selfless Greater good, simple, limited, ability to use resources (time, money, energy, people)
Surroundings	Harmonious Feeling, connections, aesthetics, litmus test, subjectivity, look	Objective Comparison, focused, objective, disconnected

	High	**Low**
Social	Altruistic Benefit provided to others, help-ori- ented, fair, sameness	Intentional Individual, growth-oriented, expectation-oriented
Power	Commanding Winning, impact, significance, growth, independent	Collaborative Team-oriented, sup- portive, contributing
Methodolo- gies	Structured Consistency, trends, methodical, proven	Receptive Flexible, adaptable, new

Remember that our driving forces tend to become our filters for what we perceive as right or wrong, how we trust, and how we feel respected; they are the source for most conflict. With that in mind, it is important to consider these when setting meaningful metrics. Otherwise we may actually avoid setting metrics, get defensive, and discount (or try to justify) the information that they provide.

Ask, "How do I know that my metric will make a difference? How will this metric increase versus decrease energy and passion?"

The Right Measure

The right measure always begins with defining the outcome you want. It is common to start by adopting existing metrics or the metrics of others. However, your metric needs to answer the question, "How will I *know* whether or not I am successful?"

Often, people spend too much effort attempting to change

behaviors that have little impact on their actual desired outcomes. Start by reviewing the new behaviors (the ways of doing things, best practices, and key accountabilities that you identified in chapter 5). With each new behavior, identify the specific results that are needed for that change to be successful.

Also, make it a practice to set a metric for each desired outcome you identified, rank them based on which is most important, and then choose the top one to three to start with. Then test them against your mission, values, vision, and guardrails, and adapt them based on what is and what is not working (refer back to what you did in chapter 2 if you need help remembering).

In his book *Human Competence: Engineering Worthy Performance*, author Thomas F. Gilbert outlines a simple five-point test[5] for ensuring that your metric is driving toward the right outcome:

- Accomplishment—You don't need to see the action, behavior, or accountability to determine its effectiveness. You should be able to simply look at the results and know that the behavior is working.
- Control—You need to be in control of the behaviors necessary to drive the result.
- Overall Objective—If the result is achieved, will anything else be expected?
- Reconcilable—If the result is accomplished perfectly, will other results be hampered?
- Numbers—Is the information valid and reliable?

My mission is to bring out the gold in people so that they impact the world. My values are faith, authenticity, wonder,

5 Thomas F. Gilbert, *Human Competence: Engineering Worthy Performance* (San Francisco: Pfeiffer, 2007).

advocacy, and impact. Therefore, all my metrics need to point to how I am pushing myself beyond what I can see, revealing authentic truth, pondering and questioning, pushing myself and others higher, and showing big impact.

When I set the goal of losing one hundred and fifty pounds, my metrics were focused on digging to the root of what was preventing me from losing weight, looking for patterns and themes that would accelerate the results, sharing my journey with others along the way, and asking lots of what-if questions as the data was revealed through the results.

If you were to look at any of my scorecards (groups of metrics for each desired change), you would see a great deal of intensity in the metrics. That is because I am an intense person, and that drives my mission and values. However, this wouldn't work for everyone. In fact, my scorecards would overwhelm most people, which is why it is so important to find metrics that are both reliable and meaningful to *you*.

Keep It Simple, Stupid (KISS)

I regularly help individuals and organizations set metrics. Usually, they are either not using them at all or the metrics are much too complicated and overwhelming. One of the best things you can do is keep it simple, stupid! This is not intended to imply that you are stupid. Rather, I am saying that it is important to start with a few basic metrics that are uncomplicated and then add or make them more complex along the way. In other words, complexity is never the goal in itself; metrics only need to grow in complexity as long as that continues to serve you well.

Also, while formal scorecards and metric-tracking tools can be helpful (especially when you have groups of people working together to achieve a common goal), metrics can be just as impactful if they are unwritten and informal. For example, I have struggled with getting stuck throughout writing this book. The way I think is very integrated and complex, so I would get overwhelmed by determining the right amount of research, practical application, and stories to include.

In the beginning I would sit for hours and not get a single word written. For months I ended up feeling frustrated, with a mind spinning full of thoughts that never made it onto paper. So I pinpointed the behavior I needed to change, which was to get more words on paper. I started by setting a goal of blocking out a day to write but quickly learned this wouldn't work. At that point I changed my metric to the number of chapters I wrote in any given sitting. Still, no progress.

Finally, I set a metric of writing for ninety minutes. I allowed myself to ride the waves of inspiration, so when I felt inspired I would sit down for ninety minutes and write in whatever chapter drove that inspiration. Wow. I found that I would look up and four hours had passed and ten thousand words were on the screen! It wasn't until I pinpointed the specific behavior that needed to change (get more words on paper) that I found a measure that would work. I didn't have to complete an entire chapter, it didn't have to be perfect, and it didn't need to be in order. I simply needed to get words on paper. And I didn't need to track that metric on a formal scorecard. I just had to sit down and commit to at least ninety minutes, when I felt inspired.

Set Leading and Lagging Indicators

Every change is identified in order to produce specific results, and to produce results, one must first change their behaviors. The definition of insanity is trying to get a different result from the same actions. However, as illustrated by the story of the Chinese bamboo, you may not be able to see or measure all desired results right away. Therefore, it is important to establish measures for both behaviors (means) and results (ends).

In the world of metrics, these are also known as leading and lagging indicators. Leading indicators say, "If I engage in these behaviors, I am likely to realize the result I desire," whereas lagging indicators say, "I am/am not realizing the result I desire." Leading indicators look forward while lagging indicators look back.

Based on my example above, a leading indicator would be, "If I spent ninety minutes writing when I feel inspired, I will likely get more words on paper," whereas a lagging indicator would be, "I wrote ten thousand words." My example showed that the lagging indicator, which was measuring the number of words I wrote, was too overwhelming for me and actually shut down my creativity. On the other hand, writing for ninety minutes when I felt inspired allowed me to get started because I know that when I get inspired, it drives energy and impact.

Both of these indicators were important for me. The leading indicator helped me get unstuck and create a new behavior of writing, while the lagging indicator allowed me to check my progress against the goal of writing approximately fifty thousand words (the benchmark for a book like this). It was important for me to recognize when I needed to use a leading indicator and when to use a lagging indicator, to get the performance I desired.

When I set metrics, I typically look for at least one leading and one lagging indicator for each behavior I am seeking to change. However, sometimes we would want to use leading indicators over lagging ones, such as when we are still trying to pinpoint the top behaviors that will drive performance, when we are a long way from our desired performance goal, when there are multiple behaviors that could impact the result, when the behaviors that need to change are sensitive or offensive, or when poor performance results are due to causes beyond our control. All change is based on a hypothesis that it will create a better life, and the way to get to that better life is also a set of hypotheses.

So, leading indicators can help identify and test the most relevant behaviors that will get you to your desired outcomes. Conversely, results-based metrics can be more effective when you are already skilled in the behavior that drives results, the behaviors and results are clearly related and proven, or results are improving. Lagging (results-based) measures are best when you have a period of time that will show trends. However, it is important that these forward- and rear-facing metrics go hand in hand to give you a glimpse of the whole picture, show you overall results, and help you adapt and pivot when necessary.

Celebrate Often and Be Prepared to Adapt

It is important to measure progress often and pivot when necessary. Changes in data will inform you when the value of your reinforced behavior is starting to lose its effect, which will allow you to continue progressing and accelerating your desired change. Often our reinforced behaviors lose their effect because we don't see the underlying results, we are fatigued from the new behaviors (and our brain is actually "hurting" from new mindsets related to those new behaviors), or the new behavior becoming "normal" results in a loss of awe and wonder with the new way of doing things.

In order to accelerate and sustain the impact of positive behavioral reinforcers, it is important to pause and celebrate often. Studies show that celebrating causes our brain to produce dopamine and other neuropeptides that are critical in the development and hardening of the new neuropathways built when we are changing mindsets and carrying out new behaviors.[6] In order to celebrate a result, we must pause and intentionally acknowledge the value that the result created. This drives even more celebration, because the more value we create and identify, the more we will tend to celebrate. It is a continuous cycle.

For that reason, it is important to regularly stop, acknowledge your progress, and celebrate how far you have come. It is an essential part of the neurological process of change. One way I do this in my own life and work is to ask, "What's working? What's not? What needs to change?" at the beginning of every planning meeting or, personally, at the beginning of every day.

Pause to Reflect and Celebrate

I hit a plateau about a year after I started my weight-loss journey. My weight loss had slowed considerably, and my body was

starting to need a new set of behaviors to get me to the next level. So, I pulled out an outfit I had worn at the beginning of my weight-loss journey and laid on top of it the outfit I was wearing that day. I took a picture as a reminder of how much of our progress we forget about. Now I pull that picture out and celebrate to encourage myself every time I am feeling down about the "lack" of progress I am seeing in my journey to health.

---

6   Demarest and Schoof, *Answering the Central Question*, 62.

In chapter 4 we talked about how as little as five to seven minutes of contemplative thought rewires our brain. So why not take just five minutes a day to reflect on and celebrate the wins you *are* having?

Gratitude

One of the primary ways you can celebrate is by intentionally practicing gratitude. When we are under stress, our brains have more than 1,400 known physical and chemical reactions going at any given time. If we stay in this state too long, nerve cells start to die off, causing us to forget the impact and value of our new change. Extreme periods of this "cell suicide" will lead to anxiety, depression, and various other illnesses.[7]

Therefore, in order for your change to be sustained, you must take the time to eliminate this stress. Gratitude does this by leading to the feeling that life is worth living, which results in resilience and the ability to adapt more quickly.

When I see something show up regularly as a key to driving meaningful and sustainable change, I dig deep into that key to understand it at its core. I did this with gratitude and unlocked some very interesting and powerful insights that changed how I thought about and practiced gratitude on a daily basis.

As I dug into the core of gratitude, I noticed that it was actually a sacrifice. A sacrifice is something that we choose to do, and it needs to cost us something. As I continued to dig into the root words for *gratitude* and *thankfulness*, I discovered several additional keys. First, both are verbs. We need to take action with them. Second, they are tied to a shifting of sorts. When we practice gratefulness, we actually get something bigger in return. Third, gratefulness requires us to open our hands to what we

---

7   Brown, *The Gifts in You*, 157.

are grateful for, being willing to let go of those very things in order to receive something new. Fourth, the root of the word means power, means, and direction. And finally, another root of the word means favor and pardon that leads to blessing and happiness.

This discovery blew my mind! What this is telling me is that if we actively practice gratefulness and are willing to let go of the very thing we are grateful for, we will receive something much bigger in return. It also tells me that we need to seek to be grateful for things that we may not even see as our current reality.

So why is gratefulness a key in a chapter on measuring results? Because it is a critical key for us to be able to let go of past results (desired or undesired) so we can take hold of something new. Gratefulness is absolutely crucial to our ability to make meaningful and sustainable change.

When Rob passed, a friend made a gratitude bowl for the kids and me. Every night at dinner we pass that bowl and each person gets the opportunity to share what they are grateful for, even in the moments when we do not particularly feel grateful. It was amazing how that simple, practical practice shifted and opened things up for our family. We were able to find joy in the middle of an excruciatingly painful and uncertain time of our lives.

After twenty years of studying and practicing positive psychology, I am not sure why this discovery struck me as so profound. Maybe what I had been teaching from my *head* had finally leaked down to my heart as we consciously chose to practice gratitude during a time when the results of my life looked so different from what I had expected.

Take a moment to think about what you are grateful for with your desired change. How does this shift the way you look at your desired change? Your current results? And the potential future results?

Declarations

In past chapters we have talked about the power of our words. Our brains respond to our spoken voice and move thoughts from being concepts, beliefs, and mindsets into habits. This habit of declaring is an extremely powerful and practical tool for being able to reinforce our results and drive our behaviors to the next level of success.

At the same time, declarations will help reduce the stress that rises up based on the fear of failure that can be attributed to measuring results. So speak, speak, speak the positive behaviors and results that you do have, as well as the future results that will come from your continuing to reinforce your positive behaviors.

Be Ready to Adapt

In chapter 5 we talked about the power of pivoting quickly when our new behaviors lose their power and value or when we start to see negative results. Too often, we hold on to old ways of doing and measuring things to the point that we lose energy and momentum, and even realize declining results. This can cause us to get stuck, plateau, or even go backward.

Meaningful measures should be able to show you when to keep going and when to adapt to a new way of doing or measuring things. It can feel like you are repeatedly circling the same mountain. However, if you take a moment to look at your circumstances, see the results you have had over time, and recognize what has changed, you will know when you are going around the same mountain (time to change) or when you are really on a different mountain with similar surroundings (time to persevere at the next level).

Two years ago, I set a professional goal to build my team to the level where I could spend at least 80 percent of my time writing, speaking, and developing a platform of tools and resources. I started down this path when Rob passed, as I was required to step back and get my health, family, and house in order. During that time, I learned that my business, my team, and myself personally were not ready to step into this vision. I found myself back at the place where I was consulting full time and spending very little time writing, speaking, or developing.

Initially, I felt like a failure. It seemed like I was circling the same mountain and could not get to my goal. However, when I paused to reflect on what *had* changed, I realized that I was not on the same mountain at all. Actually, I had been promoted to a whole new mountain! Even though my circumstances seemed the same (more consulting, less product development), I was actually writing, speaking, and developing *through* my consulting. In fact, that season allowed us to prove the concepts, tools, and resources that have become this book and the supporting platform. I could have easily looked at the results as a failure, when in reality they were really a promotion!

So what about you? How will you know if your change goals are being met?

APPLY: Key Questions & Activation

Consider the change you are desiring to make.

- What are a few key measures that would tell you that you are achieving your desired outcomes? Are they the right measures? (Point to what you accomplished? Controllable? Achieve your overall objective? Won't hamper other goals? Valid and reliable?) Are they simple? Do they look backward (lagging) and forward (leading)? Do they support your unique driving forces? Do they align to your mission, values, and vision?

- What are some intentional ways that you can practice gratitude and celebrate your progress along the way? What declarations do you need to make in order to reinforce your results along the way?
- How will you know it is time to adapt your measures as you go?
- What are one to three key takeaways from this chapter that you need to share with somebody else? Teach at least one other person about these takeaways.

Go to www.wearetheunstoppable.com to find simple and practical tools that can help you make and sustain your change.

- Download worksheets that will help you pinpoint and set meaningful metrics.
- Take an assessment to discover your unique driving forces, so you can set more relevant metrics.

Chapter 9

TRANSFORMATION BEYOND YOU

T ake a moment now to savor what you've accomplished in reading and working through this book. Really, I mean it! What you have done is truly significant. In my opinion, it is likely to be one of the most significant things you have done in your life or could do in your life. Maybe you think that's overstating things, but allow me to let you in on one of my deepest passions—legacy.

You might not know it, but one of the greatest transfers of wealth in the history of the world is about to happen all around us. It's going to happen because the Baby Boomer generation is nearing and reaching retirement age. This translates to roughly ten million businesses in the United States alone that will soon transition to new ownership, whether to a family member or someone outside the family.

That is a lot of transition, and just like any individual or organization making transitions, most of these businesses will not be ready for it when it comes. This means that millions of Boomers will reach retirement and not know how to hand off the company they built, the organization they established, their baby—their legacy.

Countless other non-business-owner Boomers will be also thinking about their own transitions. Statistically speaking, most Boomers were happy enough as long as they made money and established security for themselves, but now that they are nearing retirement, they want to know what it was all for. They are handing the fruit of their hard work to someone else, and if they're not prepared to handle that transition well, they are realizing that all their hard work might just come to nothing.

Leaving a legacy isn't just for Baby Boomers. No matter what generation you are from, you can think about the legacy you are going to leave—the future impact of each little choice and change you made as you worked your way through this transformation journey. That is why what you have done in working diligently through this book is so important, because by doing this you are preparing yourself to transition well, regardless of your generation. You are looking ahead in your life to see the changes that are coming and are working now to be ready for them. This positions you so that, at any point in your future, you will be able to look back and confidently say, "I chose the life I have lived, I am happy with it, and I am ready for what's next."

Live Intentionally to Leave a Legacy

As I reflect on the short forty-five years that Rob lived on this earth, I am overtaken by the fact that it was the intentional, little moments that had the most meaning and made the greatest impact. He had kept most of his information and passwords on a work computer that needed to be returned after he passed, so the kids and I were left with no passwords or records to any of his accounts. As well, he was a simple person who got rid of anything that wasn't giving him value in the moment, so he left behind very few *things*.

But it wasn't his information, records, or things that created the significant legacy that he left. Rather, it was the memories of the times he spent taking the kids and me to minister, feed the homeless, pray for the sick, and help anyone in need. He would have—and often did—give the shirt off his back for someone in need. It was the countless hours he spent goofing around with the kids, playing basketball with Tyler, driving Caleb to school, and taking Grace on dates and to the annual Father-Daughter Dance. It was in the late-night runs to Kwik Trip to get Sammy his favorite treat, despite his being tired from a long day at work. Our marriage wasn't perfect. In fact, much of it was very hard, but I always knew that we were in it together, that we were both committed to growing individually and as a couple.

Every year of our marriage (except one) we went away as a couple to answer many of the same questions that you answered as you journeyed through this book. We would revisit our mission, vision, and values, then we would dream about the upcoming year both individually and as a couple, landing on a written life plan for the year ahead. I still have every one of those plans. As I read through them and reflect on twenty-one years of marriage, it is amazing to see how many dreams were realized even though the way they manifested might have changed. I realize that I was living the power of intention all those years, without even knowing it!

The kids and I miss Rob here on earth, but we know with every part of our being that he intentionally lived his life in a way that will leave a powerful legacy for generations to come. My advice to you is that life is short. You don't know when you will take your last breath, so be sure to live life intentionally. What legacy are your choices leaving? What change can you make today that will transform yourself, your family, your organization, your community, and your world?

Permission to Be Imperfect

This book is many things, and perhaps two things most of all. First, it is a book that is best used regularly, rather than only read once and then left on a shelf. Like I said, Rob and I would take time away every year to walk through this and set fresh vision. Second, it is a guidebook to help you through any change or transition you have in life and, hopefully, to lead you into proactively choosing your changes and transitions so much as you are able. No life only goes through one change or transition, and each change or transition is different, but this book can help you successfully navigate all of them. That's part of why it's called *Unstoppable*.

One thing this book is not meant to be, however, is a rule book, which means you can't do the process this book outlines perfectly. In fact, there is no perfect standard for you to meet or fall short of. For there to be a perfect standard would mean we all have to be the same, so we could share the same standard. But we all have different identities, dreams, purposes, circumstances, personalities, wirings, and more. This means there is no perfection to this process; I give you permission to be imperfect!

Sometimes it is hard to get started because we want to make sure our change has the perfect conditions for success. Sometimes it is hard to get started because we are actually afraid of what will happen if we realize success. I have been reminding myself of this very thing as I have been writing the book. I am a recovering perfectionist who is wired to take responsibility for whatever I commit to; who is driven to continuously maximize, learn, and improve; and who wants to relate to and individualize whatever I do for others. Letting this book go to print and practicing the MVP principle is especially hard for me.

When I started writing this book, I questioned the amount of time, resources, and emotional investment that it would require. I asked my writing coach, David, if it was worth it. After all, everyone seems to be writing books right now. And there are hundreds of books on change! He replied, "Michelle, many people have kids, but that didn't stop you from having yours." That response reminded me that we all have our own part to play in impacting the world around us and leaving a legacy. I encourage you to not let the fear of failure or success prevent you from getting started on the transformative change that is in your heart.

The only thing we can do is stay engaged with working toward our goals. Along the way, we'll gradually become more and more of the best versions of ourselves. In the meantime, we will all be works in progress, including me. After all, I'm the one writing this book, a person who has led entire companies and organizations through this material for fifteen years, and yet my stories show that I'm still in process myself.

Becoming Unstoppable

That's why you'll want to keep this book handy and reference it regularly to continue practicing the process. As I said all the way back in chapter 1, you don't have to answer every question in every chapter, but only the ones that speak to you. When you go through this book again to help you through future transitions, you'll answer different questions than you did this time.

The whole point is that you keep progressing, not that you are perfect. Don't stop. It's okay to have hurdles. It's okay to face unforeseen obstacles. It's okay to take on difficult challenges. You will more than manage them, more than navigate them; you will overcome them!

Just keep working through the process. Walk through each

of the P's you learned in this book—Passion, Purpose, Principles, Practices, Proficiencies, Platform, and Performance. Remember the outcome you want, as it will keep you focused. Take the time to get the right mindsets; it will make your successes both possible and sustainable. Stay engaged with what drives you; it will keep you moving forward. Build your strengths and practice the right skills; it will lead to more-powerful results. Gather the right people and tools around you; they will enable you to succeed beyond your own abilities for the long haul. Measure your results; they prove you hit the right target and enable you to celebrate.

The more you engage this process, the more natural it will become. Eventually, it will simply be your new normal. This all starts with the small choices you make, like the choice to read this book, and the results will keep growing.

The Eighth P: Power

Throughout this journey, you have learned seven simple steps to getting unstuck, making big change, and unlocking your potential. However, transformation isn't just about you. We all have some sort of change that we want to make in our families, workplaces, communities, and the world.

We also talked about how transformation beyond us doesn't truly happen until we transform ourselves. However, it is when you start the journey of transforming yourself alongside others that the energy and momentum is built to really transform the world. This is truly the 8th P: Power. Just like knocking down the first domino can create enough energy to knock down a series of dominos much greater in size, collectively taking the first step toward change can create the power and momentum to catch fire, start movements, and revolutionize the world.

Going through this process with others creates a multiplying effect in each of your lives. You gain common language that reinforces the tools in this book, helping you gain each tool's full power and potential. You also walk with others who will encourage you when you are in the difficult moments of transition. But perhaps most of all, you immediately begin to meet your need for transcendence—helping others become their best—all the while building a legacy for your own life that will reach further than you ever could alone.

An African proverb says it best:

If you want to go fast, go alone.

If you want to go far, go together.

I strongly encourage you to not go through this journey alone. Grab a friend, your family, your team, or a small group, and have fun walking through this transformative journey together. Here are some ways that you can continue your own transformation and help others become unstoppable:

- Go on Instagram, Facebook, Twitter, and/or LinkedIn and talk about the impact you have received from reading this book. Use the hashtag #wearetheunstoppable.

- Give us feedback so we can continue to improve this book and the support tools and resources that will help you make transformative change. Go to www. wearetheunstoppable.com/feedback, provide feedback, and we will send you a free copy of the next edition of this book to give to someone else.

- Check out our platform of unstoppable assessments, tools, and resources at www.wearetheunstoppable.com.
- On our website, you can also sign up for an unstoppable experience, 90-Day Cohort, or one-on-one or peer coaching.

Remember, you are getting unstuck, making big change, and unlocking your potential—because you are truly unstoppable!

Acknowledgments

Writing a book is harder than I thought and more rewarding than I could have ever imagined—especially since I was writing a book about being unstoppable. As you will come to discover throughout this book, being unstoppable isn't possible if you're taking the journey alone. Countless people have come alongside me on my journey of being unstoppable. However, I would like to take a moment to recognize some key people.

First of all, none of this would have been possible without my family. Rob, you were the one who always said that it didn't matter what we were doing, we just needed to do it together and never quit. The twenty-one years we were married may not have always been easy, but I always knew that whatever came our way, we would figure it out together. Thank you for always pushing me to think bigger, run faster, and never quit.

Caleb, Tyler, Grace, and Sammy, this book is for you. My hope is that I model my life in a way that inspires you to be you, reach for the stars, and never give up. The ultimate gift in life is to know that I have left a legacy to you, your kids, and their kids.

To my family, Rob's family, and my dear friends, thank you for always being there for us. Your support and encouragement has allowed me to make it through some of best and worst times of life. This book wouldn't be a reality if you hadn't been there to help carry the load as I wrote, worked with clients, and focused on keeping things as stable as possible for the kids. Mom and Dad, I especially appreciate how you raised me to believe all things are possible, never quit, and shoot for the stars.

To my team, you are amazing. One of the greatest gifts is to spend a majority of my days with each of you. The fact that we have someone from every generation helps bring diverse perspective, understanding, and relatability with the hundreds of leaders that we serve. Thank you for believing in me, and being willing to roll up your sleeves, try new things, and run beside me as we seek to bring significant impact and legacy to leaders and business owners.

To my publishing team (David, Nathanael, Christy, Yvonne, Katherine, and the others I never knew about), thank you for helping to make this dream a reality. Your consistent encouragement when I felt discouraged and stuck (often), ability to understand my heart and voice, and amazing skill made this process so much easier than going it alone. I look forward to writing many more books with you.

To my clients, thank you for the privilege of allowing us to serve you over the years. This book would not be a reality without your being willing and open to us partnering with you as you navigate your own critical changes. My hope is that this book serves as a resource that will help you think bigger, go further, and serve as a bridge as you leave your own legacy.

Finally, thanks to my heavenly Father. I thank you for the loving gift of eternity that gives me faith in the possibility of a better tomorrow, hope to keep moving through the storms of life, and love to recognize and bring out the gold in others around me. It is because of you that I am truly unstoppable.

About the Author

As the founder of VisionOne, Michelle Bonahoom is passionate about working with mid-market business owners to increase their value, and in preparation for sale, strategic acquisitions, and transferring to the next generation of leadership. She has worked with over one hundred different companies as they prepared for key critical transitions. Over the past twenty years, Michelle has accumulated diverse experience as a business owner, private investor, consultant, and advocate for mid-market companies who are seeking to stabilize, achieve added value, reach high-performance results, and leave a legacy for the next generation.

Michelle has a BS in International Business and an MBA in Entrepreneurship and Private Equity, and has earned an integrated set of value-growth certifications in mergers and acquisitions, strategic development and execution, performance management, and positive and organizational psychology. This broad set of experience and credentials has proven to be critical when working with business owners to successfully turn around, grow, and transition their businesses.

Michelle is passionate about giving back. She invests in her community through nonprofit board service, through teaching leadership, entrepreneurship, and self-discovery through her church, and as an adjunct professor for several community colleges. She loves to spend her free time with her family, reading and dreaming, and advocating for emerging leaders.

VisionOnePerformance.com

WeAreTheUnstoppable.com